The Candidate's Handbook: A Practical Guide to Winning Elections

Dedication

This book is dedicated to the countless unsung heroes of political campaigns—the volunteers who knock on doors in the pouring rain, the phone bankers who tirelessly make calls, the social media managers who craft compelling narratives, and the finance teams who meticulously manage resources. It is to those individuals, often working long hours for little compensation, whose unwavering dedication and commitment make the democratic process possible.
Their passion, resilience, and belief in the power of their candidate and their cause inspire us all. This work is a small tribute to their tireless efforts, a recognition of the crucial role they play in shaping our political landscape, and a testament to the enduring power of grassroots activism in a world increasingly dominated by digital technologies. It is for them that this guide is written, with the hope that it will equip them with the tools and knowledge to run even more effective and successful campaigns. May this handbook serve as a guide for them

to work smarter, not harder, towards a future where campaigns are run efficiently, with maximum impact, and with the utmost integrity. This dedication extends also to the many
candidates, past and present, who bravely put themselves forward for public service, facing criticism and scrutiny, navigating complex electoral landscapes, and dedicating themselves to serving the
interests of their communities. Their courage, perseverance and commitment to public service are a constant inspiration and a
reminder of the importance of civic engagement. This book is a resource for them, empowering them to effectively translate their vision into action and impact the lives of those they represent. To all who strive to make a difference through political action, this book is humbly dedicated.

Preface

Winning a political campaign is a complex undertaking, requiring a multifaceted approach and a deep understanding of the political landscape. This book is not simply a theoretical exploration of campaign strategies; it's a practical, hands-on guide designed to equip you with the tools and knowledge you need to succeed. My extensive experience as a political strategist and campaign manager has shown me time and again that even the most brilliant ideas fail if not properly executed. This book focuses on bridging the gap between theory and practice, providing step-by-step instructions, actionable strategies, and real-world examples to guide you through every stage of the campaign process. Whether you're a seasoned campaign manager or a first-time candidate, you'll find valuable insights and practical advice within these pages. From the initial legal and financial groundwork to the development of a winning campaign message and the effective implementation of grassroots outreach, this comprehensive guide covers all the essential elements of a successful campaign. I've consciously avoided overwhelming you with complex political theory or jargon. Instead, the tone is conversational and approachable, designed to empower you with confidence and clarity as you navigate the challenges of electoral politics. Within these pages you will find a clear roadmap to success—a practical and accessible guide for anyone seeking to run a truly effective campaign, one that builds genuine connections with voters and translates its campaign vision into tangible results. The

information contained in this book is the result of countless hours of research, analysis of successful campaigns and real-world experience on the front lines. Remember that while this book offers valuable insights, each campaign is unique; adapt the strategies outlined within these pages to your specific circumstances and the demands of your unique political environment. Good luck, and may your campaign be a resounding success.

Introduction

The political landscape is constantly evolving, making it more challenging than ever to run a successful campaign. The traditional methods of campaigning are still relevant, but they need to be complemented by a comprehensive digital strategy and a deep understanding of the modern voter. This book serves as your comprehensive guide to navigating the complexities of the modern political campaign, providing a step-by-step approach that incorporates both proven techniques and cutting-edge strategies. This book is not merely a compilation of information; it's a practical toolkit designed to be used from the initial stages of campaign planning through to election day and beyond. Whether you're a novice candidate taking your first steps into the political arena or a seasoned politician looking to refine your approach, you'll find valuable insights and actionable advice within these pages.

We'll explore the fundamental aspects of campaign management, including the crucial legal and financial setup, the establishment of a strong online presence, the development and implementation of effective fundraising strategies, the crafting of a compelling campaign
message, and the effective execution of grassroots outreach efforts. This guide delves into the importance of digital marketing, showing you how to leverage social media, email marketing, and online advertising to reach voters and build your campaign's reach.
Furthermore, you will discover the secrets to cultivating high-value donors, organizing successful fundraising events, and effectively managing your campaign finances. This book also provides practical guidance on organizing your campaign team, including defining roles, fostering effective communication, and managing volunteers.
We will also discuss critical elements such as crafting persuasive campaign literature, effectively responding to opponent attacks, and mastering the art of public speaking. Finally, we will look at what to do after the election, with advice on conducting post-election
analysis, planning for future campaigns and maintaining engagement with your constituents. This guide offers a blend of

proven methods and innovative strategies to help candidates at all levels achieve victory. So, let's embark on this journey to building a powerful, effective campaign – one step at a time.

A StepbyStep Guide

Before embarking on the exhilarating, yet often daunting, journey of a political campaign, a solid legal and financial foundation is
paramount. This forms the bedrock upon which your entire campaign will be built. Neglecting this crucial first step can lead to significant complications, even jeopardizing the entire endeavor. This chapter focuses on establishing that foundation, starting with the formation of your Federal Election Commission (FEC) committee. This is not a mere formality; it's a legally mandated step with significant
consequences for compliance and the overall success of your
campaign.

Forming your FEC committee is akin to laying the cornerstone of a house. You wouldn't start constructing walls and a roof before ensuring a secure foundation. Similarly, navigating the complexities of campaign finance laws requires the establishment of a legally sound FEC committee. This section provides a detailed, step-by-step guide to assist you in this critical process. Remember, accuracy and meticulous attention to detail are essential here, as any errors can lead to hefty fines and potential legal challenges.

The first step involves understanding the types of committees you can form. The most common type for candidates is a Principal Campaign Committee (PCC). This is the primary committee responsible for raising and spending money directly in support of your candidacy. Other types, such as authorized committees and independent expenditure-only committees, have different rules and regulations and may be relevant depending on your campaign's structure and fundraising strategy. Familiarize yourself with the FEC's website (www.fec.gov) – it's your bible during this phase.

Next, you'll need to register your committee with the FEC. This involves completing the Statement of Candidacy (FEC Form 2) if you are a candidate, and FEC Form 1 (Registration Statement) if you are forming a committee that supports or opposes a candidate without being directly affiliated with them. The forms are fairly

comprehensive and require accurate
information about your

committee's purpose, officers, and treasurer. The treasurer is a crucial role; they are legally responsible for managing the committee's finances and ensuring compliance with all applicable regulations. Choose this individual carefully; their understanding of campaign finance laws is critical.

The FEC website offers detailed instructions and downloadable versions of these forms. Take your time to complete them accurately. Inaccurate information will cause delays and potentially lead to rejection of your application. Many candidates find it helpful to seek assistance from legal counsel specializing in campaign finance. The initial investment in professional guidance can prevent far greater expenses and headaches down the line. Think of it as an insurance policy against costly mistakes.

Once the forms are completed, you'll need to submit them to the FEC. You can do this electronically or by mail, as specified on the FEC website. Keep copies of everything. Organize a detailed filing system from the outset – you'll need to track all your paperwork throughout the entire campaign. The FEC provides a confirmation upon successful registration, which acts as your official committee identification number. This number is crucial for all future financial transactions and reporting.

After your committee is registered, you'll need to open a separate bank account dedicated solely to campaign funds. This is non-negotiable. Mingling campaign funds with personal funds is a major violation of campaign finance laws and can result in severe penalties. Most banks are familiar with the requirements for campaign accounts and will guide you through the process. Ensure that the bank account is clearly identified as belonging to your FEC committee, using the official committee name and ID number.

Another critical step is obtaining an Employer Identification Number (EIN) from the Internal Revenue Service (IRS). This is similar to a Social Security number but for your committee. You'll need the EIN to open the bank account and to file tax returns. The IRS provides a simple online application process to obtain an EIN; it is typically processed within minutes. Make sure to keep a record of your EIN; it's as important as your committee's FEC identification number.

Maintaining meticulous financial records is crucial throughout the entire campaign. This is not simply a matter of good bookkeeping; it's a legal requirement. The FEC mandates detailed reporting of all income and expenses. Keep detailed receipts for every transaction, from postage to catering for campaign events. Use accounting software designed specifically for political campaigns if possible —this will help you categorize transactions accurately and simplify the reporting process.

Regular reporting to the FEC is a fundamental aspect of campaign finance compliance. This involves submitting periodic reports outlining all income and expenses. The reporting deadlines are clearly defined on the FEC website. Missing deadlines can result in significant fines. You are required to file various reports, including pre-election reports, post-election reports, and potentially other

reports depending on the size and scope of
your campaign.
Understanding these reporting requirements is non-
negotiable.

Proactive compliance is your best strategy.
Don't wait until the last minute to complete
these reports. Establish a routine for
financial record-keeping and reporting
from the very beginning. Consider enlisting
the help of a professional accountant or
campaign finance consultant to assist with
this aspect of the campaign. Their expertise
can prevent costly mistakes and ensure that
your campaign remains compliant with all
applicable regulations.

Remember, navigating the legal and
financial aspects of a political campaign
can be intricate. The FEC website is an
invaluable
resource, but don't hesitate to seek
professional advice when needed. The
peace of mind that comes from knowing
you're in compliance is worth the
investment. A solid legal and financial
foundation ensures that your campaign can
focus its energy where it matters most:
reaching out to voters and sharing your
vision for the future. By completing these
initial steps diligently, you lay a robust
foundation for a successful and legally
compliant political campaign. The effort

you invest in this foundational stage will
pay dividends throughout

the entire election cycle. Building a strong, legal and financially sound campaign sets the stage for success. Don't overlook this crucial first step.

Establishing a Campaign Bank Account and Obtaining an EIN

Having established your Federal Election Commission (FEC) committee, the next crucial step in building your campaign's foundation is establishing a dedicated campaign bank account and obtaining an Employer Identification Number (EIN). These
seemingly administrative tasks are, in reality, cornerstones of a legally sound and financially transparent campaign. Ignoring them can lead to significant legal and logistical hurdles, potentially derailing your entire effort before it even gains momentum.

A separate campaign bank account is not just a good idea; it's a necessity. Mingling campaign funds with personal funds is a recipe for disaster, inviting confusion, potential legal challenges, and even accusations of impropriety. A dedicated account ensures clear separation, facilitating easy tracking of income and expenses, a critical aspect of complying with FEC regulations. Moreover, it simplifies the auditing process, a process you will inevitably face. Think of it as establishing a transparent, auditable financial record for your campaign, providing a clear trail of all monetary transactions. This transparency builds public trust and protects you from potential legal pitfalls.

Choosing the right financial institution is also a significant consideration. While you might be comfortable with your personal bank, consider a bank with experience handling political campaigns. Some banks specialize in this area, offering specialized services and a deeper understanding of the unique regulatory requirements involved. They can often provide valuable guidance on best practices for managing campaign finances and ensuring compliance. Inquire about their fees, online banking capabilities, and their experience working with political campaigns. A robust online banking system will streamline your financial management, enabling you to track transactions, generate reports, and reconcile accounts efficiently.

Opening the account requires certain documentation. This will typically

include your FEC registration
information, articles of

incorporation (if applicable), and the EIN, which we will discuss in detail shortly. Be prepared to provide identification documents for the authorized signatories on the account. The bank will likely require information about the campaign's purpose, anticipated income levels, and projected expenses. Be precise and accurate in providing this information, as discrepancies can lead to delays in account activation. Remember, it's crucial to maintain meticulous records from the very beginning. This means keeping copies of all bank statements, deposit slips, and canceled checks. A well-organized filing system will be invaluable as the campaign progresses.

Now, let's turn our attention to the Employer Identification Number (EIN), also known as a Federal Tax Identification Number. This is a unique nine-digit number assigned by the Internal Revenue Service (IRS) to businesses and other entities. In the context of a political campaign, the EIN acts as your campaign's social security number for tax purposes. It's essential for filing campaign finance

reports, opening the campaign bank
account, and handling various financial
transactions related to your campaign.
Obtaining an EIN is a
relatively straightforward process, typically
completed online through the IRS website.

The application process for an EIN is quick
and free. You'll need to provide basic
information about your campaign, including
its name and address, as well as the name
and contact details of the campaign treasurer
or designated financial officer. Ensure all the
information is accurate and consistent with
the details you provided to the FEC.
Inconsistencies here can create significant
problems down the line. Once you've
completed the online application, the IRS
will typically issue your EIN instantly.
You'll receive confirmation via email, and
this confirmation will contain your unique
nine-digit EIN. Keep this information safe
and secure. It's a crucial piece of information
for all your campaign's financial dealings.

Failing to obtain an EIN before engaging in
financial activities related to your
campaign can result in significant penalties.
The IRS takes compliance seriously, and
neglecting this crucial step can lead to
delays in processing your campaign finance
reports, potentially

creating problems with the FEC as well. In addition to the potential financial penalties, the perception of non-compliance can damage your campaign's credibility and public trust. Therefore, securing your EIN should be among your highest priorities during the initial setup phase.

The EIN is more than just a tax requirement; it is a key component of establishing your campaign's identity in the financial world. It allows your campaign to function as a legitimate entity, engaging in financial transactions and complying with all necessary reporting requirements. Think of it as your campaign's official identifier, essential for opening accounts, paying vendors, and making the necessary disclosures as required by law. Without it, you would find it significantly more difficult, if not impossible, to conduct basic campaign financial operations.

Furthermore, it's essential to understand the difference between your personal finances and your campaign finances. The EIN helps maintain this critical distinction. By maintaining separate accounts and using the EIN for all campaign-related financial

activities, you're not only ensuring legal compliance but also protecting your personal assets from any potential liabilities related to the campaign. This separation of financial activities is crucial for protecting your personal finances and ensuring your campaign's financial
transparency. A transparent financial record fosters public trust and strengthens the campaign's ethical standing.

Once you have both your campaign bank account and your EIN, you are ready to commence your fundraising efforts. This separation ensures that you can clearly track all contributions and expenditures associated with your political campaign, making it much simpler to prepare and submit the necessary financial reports to the appropriate authorities. Remember, transparency is key to building public trust and maintaining a successful, ethically sound campaign.

Beyond the legal and financial aspects, obtaining an EIN
demonstrates preparedness and professionalism. It shows that your campaign is serious, organized, and committed to operating within the established legal framework. This perception can favorably

influence potential donors, volunteers, and supporters. They're more likely to trust and support a campaign that demonstrates a high level of organization and adherence to the law.

In conclusion, establishing a separate campaign bank account and obtaining an EIN are not mere formalities; they are essential steps for building a robust, legally sound, and financially transparent political campaign. By diligently completing these steps, you ensure
compliance with FEC regulations, protect your personal finances, and create a foundation for a successful and credible campaign. The time spent on these crucial initial tasks will prove invaluable as your campaign progresses, freeing you to focus your energy on the vital task of connecting with voters and achieving your electoral goals.
Remember to consult legal and financial professionals if you have any doubts or require further clarification. Their expertise can be invaluable in navigating the complexities of campaign finance and ensuring you're operating within the bounds of the law. The peace of mind that comes

with knowing your campaign is legally
compliant is an invaluable asset that will
allow you to focus your attention where it
truly matters – winning the election.

Budgeting and Financial Planning for Your Campaign

Building a successful political campaign requires more than just a compelling message and a strong team; it demands meticulous
financial planning. A well-defined budget acts as the roadmap for your campaign, guiding resource allocation and ensuring you stay within legal limits while maximizing your impact. Ignoring this crucial element can lead to financial instability, hindering your ability to execute your strategies effectively and potentially jeopardizing your chances of winning. Therefore, creating a realistic and
comprehensive budget is paramount from the very outset.

The first step in budgeting is to conduct a thorough assessment of your anticipated expenses. This involves a detailed breakdown of all potential costs, categorized for better management and analysis.
These categories might include:

Personnel Costs:
This is often the largest expense. Consider salaries for your campaign manager, field organizers, communications
director, finance director, and any other staff members. Include payroll taxes, benefits, and any other associated employment costs. Be realistic about the number of staff you need and the salaries you can afford, aiming for a balance between efficiency and cost-effectiveness. Don't underestimate the value of volunteer support, but factor in the costs of their necessary resources and training.

Advertising and Marketing:
This encompasses a wide range of activities, from digital advertising (Google Ads, social media
campaigns) to print materials (flyers, brochures, yard signs), radio and television spots, and potentially even billboard advertising. Develop a detailed media plan that outlines your target audiences, the channels you'll utilize, and the anticipated cost of each. Remember to factor in the costs of design, production, and distribution. Consider A/B testing different versions of your advertisements to optimize their effectiveness.

Fundraising Expenses:
Raising money takes money. Factor in the

costs associated with fundraising events, direct mail solicitations, online fundraising platforms, and any related administrative tasks. The cost of database management, email marketing, and event planning should be included here.

Travel and Logistics:
Campaigning often involves extensive travel. Include costs for transportation (flights, rental cars, gas), accommodation, and per diem expenses for staff and volunteers. If you plan on holding rallies or large-scale events, factor in venue rental fees, security costs, and catering.

Technology and Software:
This includes the costs associated with software subscriptions (email marketing platforms, CRM systems, fundraising platforms), website development and maintenance, and any necessary hardware purchases. Consider cloud-based solutions to reduce upfront investment costs and to allow for easier team collaboration.

Printing and Materials:
This category includes the costs of printing

campaign materials such as brochures, flyers, posters, yard signs, and any other printed materials. Don't underestimate the amount of materials you will need, especially if you're campaigning in a large area.

Polling and Research:
Conducting polls and voter surveys can provide invaluable insights into your campaign's standing and inform your strategy. Factor in these expenses early on to ensure you can gauge public opinion effectively.

Legal and Consulting Fees:
This will cover legal counsel related to campaign finance, compliance issues, and any potential legal
challenges. It might also include consulting fees for experts in various fields, such as communications, strategy, or data analysis.

Office Space and Utilities:
If you need office space, factor in rent, utilities, and other related costs. Consider co-working spaces or virtual offices as more budget-friendly alternatives.

Once you've compiled a comprehensive list of expenses, it's time to estimate the cost of each item as realistically as possible.

Overestimating is better than
underestimating, as unforeseen
expenses are a common occurrence in
political campaigns. It is crucial to
build contingency reserves into your
budget to
accommodate these unexpected costs.

Identifying potential funding sources is equally
crucial.
Diversification is key; rely on multiple
streams rather than depending solely on one
major source. Explore avenues such as:

Individual Donors:
Cultivate relationships with potential
donors through targeted outreach and
engaging communications. Craft
compelling donor prospectuses that clearly
articulate your
campaign's message and financial needs.
Explore online fundraising platforms like
WinRed (Republican) and Anedot (non-
partisan), which can streamline the
donation process.

Political Action Committees (PACs):
Explore opportunities for endorsements
and financial support from PACs aligned

with your political ideology and campaign goals. Remember to comply fully with all relevant campaign finance regulations.

Small-Dollar Donations:
Organize grassroots fundraising efforts to attract a wide base of small-dollar donors. Employ online fundraising tools to facilitate easy contributions and maintain a constant dialogue with your donor base.

Events and Fundraisers:
Host fundraising events – from intimate dinners to large rallies – to directly solicit donations and garner support.

Grants and Foundations:
Explore opportunities for grants from organizations that support candidates and causes aligned with your campaign.

Personal Funds:
Be transparent about your personal contribution to your campaign. Clearly state the amount of your personal funds invested and ensure all contributions are legally documented and reported.

Once you have a solid estimate of your expenses and a realistic projection of your income, you can create a balanced budget. This budget should be regularly reviewed and updated to reflect changing circumstances. It is imperative to maintain accurate and transparent financial records throughout the entire campaign. This not only ensures compliance with campaign finance regulations but also allows you to make informed decisions about resource allocation.

Tracking income and expenses is not just a matter of compliance; it's a crucial strategic tool. Employ a robust accounting system – either a dedicated campaign finance software or a spreadsheet program – to accurately record all financial transactions. Regularly reconcile your bank statements to ensure accuracy. Be meticulous in documenting every expense, attaching receipts and invoices as supporting documentation. This will be invaluable in case of audits or reviews.

Transparency is vital for building trust with donors and the public. Regularly publish campaign finance reports that are easily accessible to the public. This demonstrates your commitment to accountability and good governance. Employ a qualified accountant or financial advisor familiar with campaign finance regulations to ensure your financial records are accurate and compliant with all applicable laws.

Failing to plan properly financially can cripple a campaign's effectiveness, regardless of how compelling its message. A well-structured budget, coupled with proactive fundraising and diligent financial management, provides a crucial bedrock for a successful election campaign. The investment in time and effort spent on financial planning is an investment in your campaign's overall success – a foundation upon which you can build a strong and resilient race to victory. Remember, every dollar counts, and every dollar spent should contribute directly to your campaign's strategic objectives.

Understanding Campaign Finance Regulations

Navigating the complex world of campaign finance regulations is crucial for any political campaign, regardless of scale or ambition. Failure to comply with these laws can lead to significant fines, legal challenges, and even the disqualification of a candidate. This section provides a practical guide to understanding and adhering to these regulations at the federal, state, and local levels. We'll focus on the practical application of these laws, providing clear examples to help you avoid common pitfalls.

At the federal level, the Federal Election Campaign Act of 1971 (FECA), as amended, forms the cornerstone of campaign finance law. The FECA establishes strict rules regarding the disclosure of campaign contributions and expenditures, limits on individual and political action committee (PAC) contributions, and regulations on independent expenditures. The Federal

Election Commission (FEC) is responsible for enforcing these regulations. Understanding the FEC's role and the intricacies of FECA is paramount.

One of the most critical aspects of FECA is the requirement for disclosure. Campaigns must meticulously track and report all contributions and expenditures exceeding a certain threshold. This involves maintaining detailed records of donors, the amounts they contributed, and the dates of those contributions. Similarly, all campaign expenditures must be documented, including the purpose of the expenditure, the vendor involved, and the date of the payment. These records must be readily available for audits by the FEC.
Failure to maintain accurate and complete records is a serious offense that can result in significant penalties.

The contribution limits established by FECA are designed to prevent undue influence by wealthy individuals or groups. These limits specify the maximum amount an individual can contribute to a
candidate's campaign, a PAC, or a political party. These limits are adjusted periodically to account for inflation. Understanding these limits and ensuring your campaign adheres to them is non-negotiable. Exceeding these limits can lead to serious legal repercussions.

Moreover, the regulations surrounding
"soft money" contributions, which were
once a significant source of campaign
funding, have been significantly restricted.
Soft money, essentially unregulated
contributions given to political parties
rather than individual
candidates, is now largely prohibited,
underlining the importance of strict
adherence to FECA guidelines.

Beyond individual contributions, PACs play
a significant role in campaign finance. PACs
are organizations established by
corporations, labor unions, or other groups
to raise and spend money to support or
oppose political candidates. The FECA
regulates the contributions and expenditures
of PACs, limiting the amounts they can
contribute to individual candidates and
requiring them to disclose their donors and
expenditures. Coordinating with PACs
requires careful attention to detail to ensure
compliance with all applicable regulations.
Understanding the boundaries of permitted
collaboration is essential. Any appearance of
coordination that goes beyond what is
legally permissible can lead to serious legal
consequences.

Independent expenditures, which are not coordinated with a
candidate's campaign, are also subject to regulation under FECA. These expenditures, often made by Super PACs or other independent groups, can be significant, and while not directly coordinated, they are still subject to disclosure requirements. Understanding the difference between coordinated and independent expenditures is vital. The line between the two can be blurry, and unintentional violations can easily occur. Seeking legal counsel specialized in campaign finance is highly recommended to navigate these complex aspects.

While the FECA provides the framework for federal campaign finance regulations, it's essential to remember that states and localities also have their own campaign finance laws. These laws can vary significantly, so it's crucial to understand the specific regulations in your jurisdiction. For instance, some states have stricter contribution limits than the federal government, or they may regulate the use of certain types of advertising differently. Ignoring state and local laws can lead to additional penalties and complications. A comprehensive understanding of state campaign finance laws is as important as understanding the federal ones. This often requires researching the relevant state election board's website and possibly seeking legal advice specific to that state.

The process of complying with campaign finance regulations can seem daunting, but it's made significantly easier with proactive planning and careful record-keeping. From the moment you begin raising funds, you should establish a robust system for tracking all contributions and expenditures. This typically involves using specialized campaign finance software or engaging a professional campaign treasurer who is well-versed in these regulations. Accurate and detailed records are not merely a legal requirement; they are also essential for effective campaign budgeting and financial management. Knowing exactly where your money is coming from and where it's going allows for efficient resource allocation and effective strategic decision-making.

The consequences of non-compliance with campaign finance regulations can be severe. The FEC can

impose significant fines, and in extreme cases, a candidate could even be disqualified from the election. Furthermore, violations can damage a campaign's
reputation, eroding public trust and potentially impacting voter support. This makes seeking legal counsel an investment, not an expense. A campaign finance lawyer can provide invaluable
guidance in navigating the intricacies of these laws, helping you to establish compliant systems, review your records for accuracy, and prepare for potential audits.

In addition to the legal ramifications, neglecting campaign finance regulations can also hinder a campaign's overall effectiveness.
Spending too much time wrestling with administrative compliance issues diverts resources and energy away from core campaign
activities, such as voter outreach and message development. By proactively addressing these regulations, you ensure your campaign can focus on what truly matters: winning the election. This requires a proactive approach, beginning well before the campaign officially launches.

Moreover, transparency in campaign finance promotes public trust.
When voters can easily access information about a campaign's funding sources and expenditures, it helps to ensure accountability and reduces the perception of corruption or undue influence. This transparency also builds credibility with donors, who are more likely to contribute to campaigns they perceive as ethical and well-
managed. Therefore, a robust approach to campaign finance
compliance isn't simply about avoiding penalties; it's a crucial element of building a successful and credible campaign.

In summary, understanding and adhering to campaign finance
regulations is a fundamental aspect of running a successful political campaign. It requires meticulous attention to detail, proactive
planning, and the use of appropriate tools and resources. By
prioritizing compliance from the outset, your campaign can avoid legal pitfalls, maintain a strong reputation, and focus on the core tasks of winning the election. The

seemingly complex world of campaign finance laws is manageable with a strategic approach, thorough record-keeping, and, when necessary, the guidance of experienced legal counsel. Remember, this is not just about avoiding penalties; it's about building a campaign grounded in integrity and transparency, which ultimately enhances your chances of success. Proactive compliance, meticulous record-keeping and a commitment to transparency will serve as a solid foundation for a successful and ethical campaign.

Building a Strong Campaign Team

Building a successful political campaign is not a solo endeavor. Even the most charismatic candidate needs a strong, well-organized team to translate their vision into reality. This team acts as the engine of the campaign, driving fundraising, voter outreach, communication, and all the essential tasks that culminate in election day. Assembling the right team, with clearly defined roles and responsibilities, and fostering effective communication are crucial for success. A poorly managed team can lead to inefficiency, internal conflicts, and
ultimately, defeat. Conversely, a cohesive, highly functioning team can overcome obstacles and achieve remarkable results.

The size and structure of your campaign team will depend on the scale of your campaign—a local council race will require a smaller, more nimble team than a statewide gubernatorial bid. However, certain core roles remain essential regardless of scope. Let's explore these key positions and the qualities you should seek in your team members.

First, you need a
Campaign Manager
. This is the individual who oversees all aspects of the campaign, acting as the central coordinator and decision-maker. They are responsible for developing and implementing the overall strategy, managing the budget, and overseeing the work of all other team members. A successful campaign manager possesses exceptional organizational skills, strategic thinking, problem-solving abilities, and the capacity to manage diverse personalities and competing priorities. Experience in previous campaigns is highly valuable, and you should look for someone who is not just organized and capable but also possesses a demonstrated track record of success. The campaign manager is the conductor of the orchestra, ensuring that every instrument plays in harmony to create a winning symphony.

Next, you need a
Finance Director
. This role goes beyond simply balancing the books. The Finance Director is responsible for creating and managing the campaign's budget, overseeing fundraising efforts,

tracking expenses, and ensuring compliance with all applicable

campaign finance regulations. This
individual needs to be
meticulous, detail-oriented, and have a
strong understanding of financial
management principles. Transparency and
accountability are critical; this individual
must be able to provide regular, clear
financial reports to the candidate and
other key team members.
Furthermore, they need to be adept at
working with donors and understanding
the complexities of campaign finance
laws, avoiding potential legal pitfalls. A
skilled Finance Director can transform a
meager budget into an effective resource
through clever budgeting and strategic
fundraising.

A strong
Communications Director
is also paramount. This role focuses on
crafting and disseminating the campaign's
message
through various channels—press releases,
social media, advertising, and direct mail.
The Communications Director needs
excellent writing and communication skills,
and a deep understanding of media relations.
They'll be responsible for building and

maintaining positive relationships with journalists and media outlets, responding to media inquiries, and crafting compelling messaging that resonates with voters. In today's digital age, proficiency in social media marketing and online communication strategies is absolutely essential. A well-crafted communication strategy can shape public perception,
influence voter opinions, and help define the narrative surrounding the campaign.

The

Field Director
is responsible for the on-the-ground campaign efforts. This involves recruiting, training, and managing volunteers, organizing canvassing efforts, coordinating phone banks, and
overseeing get-out-the-vote (GOTV) activities. Strong leadership qualities, organizational skills, and the ability to motivate and
manage a large team of volunteers are essential. The Field Director is the boots-on-the-ground leader, ensuring that the campaign reaches out to voters directly, builds grassroots support, and drives voter turnout on election day. Their ability to build and maintain a
motivated, well-organized field team is critical to success.

Depending on the campaign's resources and the specific needs, you may also need specialists in areas such as:

Digital Marketing:

Managing the campaign's online presence, including website development, social media marketing, and online advertising. This requires expertise in SEO, social media platforms, and digital advertising campaigns. A successful digital strategist can leverage data analytics to maximize impact and reach targeted demographics.

Fundraising:

While some fundraising responsibility falls under the Finance Director, a dedicated fundraising professional may be necessary for larger campaigns. This individual would develop and implement strategies for attracting high-value donors, cultivating relationships with potential contributors, and managing donor communications. They would understand the nuances of donor prospectuses and donor cultivation.

Legal Counsel:

Having an attorney specializing in election law is crucial. They advise on campaign finance regulations, compliance issues, and potential legal challenges. This is an essential role for

ensuring the campaign operates within
the bounds of the law.

Pollster:
Pollsters provide data-driven insights into
voter preferences and opinions, shaping
campaign strategies and messaging. Their
role is critical in gauging the effectiveness of
the campaign's outreach and adapting
strategies as needed.

Press Secretary:
In large campaigns, a dedicated Press
Secretary handles media relations, press
conferences, and daily communication with
the press, often managing the candidate's
public image.

Beyond the specific roles, successful
campaign teams share several key
characteristics. Effective communication is
paramount. Regular meetings, clear
communication channels, and a
collaborative
atmosphere are essential. Regular briefings
should ensure that every member
understands the campaign's goals,
strategies, and their individual
contributions. Building a team culture of
mutual respect, trust, and cooperation is
fundamental for success.

Team building activities can help solidify relationships and foster a strong team identity. These activities need not be extravagant; simple team lunches, informal gatherings, or shared volunteer experiences can create a strong team bond. It is crucial to address conflicts quickly and constructively, fostering an environment where open communication and problem-solving are the norm, not the exception.

Effective leadership is equally important. The campaign manager should foster a positive and productive work environment,
empowering team members, providing clear direction, and offering constructive feedback. Regular performance reviews, both formal and informal, can help maintain high performance and address any issues proactively. Recognizing and rewarding individual and team accomplishments fosters morale and strengthens team cohesion.
Leading by example is essential: a committed and hardworking
campaign manager inspires their team to follow suit.

Finally, remember that building a campaign team is an ongoing process. As the campaign progresses, you may need to adjust the team's structure and responsibilities to meet evolving needs. Regular assessment and adaptation are vital. The ability to adapt to changing circumstances and build flexibility into the team structure is critical for successfully navigating the dynamic nature of a political

campaign. A strong, well-managed campaign team is the cornerstone of a successful election bid. Investing time and effort in building such a team pays dividends in efficiency, morale, and ultimately, victory.

Creating a Professional Campaign Website

Creating a compelling and effective campaign website is crucial in today's digital age. It serves as the central hub for your campaign, providing voters and potential supporters with easy access to information about your candidacy, platform, and events. A well-designed website not only enhances your campaign's image but also plays a vital role in boosting your online presence and reaching a wider audience. Ignoring this aspect is akin to fighting a battle without a map—you might stumble upon some victories, but a comprehensive strategy will always yield far better results. This section will guide you through the process of building a professional campaign website that effectively communicates your message and drives engagement.

First, you need a clear understanding of your target audience. Who are you trying to reach? What are their concerns? What kind of information are they looking for? Answering these questions will help you tailor your website's content and design to resonate with your specific voters. For example, a campaign targeting younger voters might benefit from a more visually dynamic website with interactive elements, while a campaign focused on older voters might prioritize clear, concise text and easy navigation.

The domain name is your digital address, so choose wisely. Select a domain name that is easy to remember, reflects your campaign brand, and includes relevant keywords. For example, if your name is John Smith and you're running for mayor, "JohnSmithForMayor.com" or a similar variation would be ideal. Avoid using overly complicated or difficult-to-spell names. Check the availability of your preferred domain name through a domain registrar like GoDaddy or Namecheap. Consider securing variations of your preferred name to prevent competitors from registering similar domains.

Once you have secured your domain name, you need to choose a website platform. There are numerous options available, ranging from simple website builders like Wix or Squarespace to more sophisticated content management systems (CMS) like WordPress.

Website builders offer user-friendly interfaces and pre-designed templates, making them ideal for those without prior web
development experience. WordPress, on the other hand, offers greater flexibility and customization options but requires some technical knowledge or the assistance of a web developer. The choice will depend on your budget, technical skills, and the level of customization required.

The design of your website is paramount. It should be visually
appealing, easy to navigate, and mobile-friendly. A cluttered or confusing website will quickly turn away potential visitors. Ensure that your website loads quickly, as slow loading times can
significantly impact user experience. Use high-quality images and videos to enhance the visual appeal of your site and make it more engaging. Maintain a consistent brand identity throughout the
website, utilizing your campaign's logo, color scheme, and fonts. Remember, your website is an extension of your campaign's brand. A professional and well-designed website will leave a positive

impression on visitors and boost your credibility.

Key content elements for your website include a clear and concise "About" page introducing your candidacy, your platform outlining your key policy positions, a "News" or "Blog" section featuring press releases, updates, and event announcements, an "Events" calendar showcasing your upcoming appearances and rallies, and a "Contact" page with clear instructions on how potential supporters can get in touch. Additionally, incorporate a prominent call to action—
encouraging visitors to volunteer, donate, or sign up for your email list. Strategic placement of these calls to action is crucial to driving engagement and achieving your campaign's objectives.

Search Engine Optimization (SEO) is critical for ensuring that your website appears high in search engine results. This involves
optimizing your website's content and structure to improve its ranking in search results for relevant keywords. Research keywords related to your campaign and incorporate them naturally into your website's content. Use descriptive titles and meta descriptions for your website pages. Ensure that your website is mobile-

friendly, as a significant percentage of
internet users access websites via mobile

devices. Regularly update your website's content with fresh, relevant material, as search engines favor websites that are frequently
updated.

Consider integrating a secure online donation platform directly into your website, enabling supporters to make contributions easily and securely. Platforms like Stripe or PayPal offer secure payment
processing services. Make sure to comply with all relevant campaign finance laws and regulations when processing donations. Transparency is key, and clearly outlining your donation policies on your website will build trust with your supporters. Consider providing different donation levels to cater to various giving
capacities.

Beyond the core content, explore the possibility of adding interactive elements to enhance engagement. For example, you could
incorporate a volunteer signup form, a social media feed, or a map showing the location of your upcoming events. Interactive elements make the website more dynamic and

engaging, encouraging visitors to spend
more time exploring your campaign's online
presence.

Regularly update your website with fresh
content to keep it engaging and current. This
not only helps with SEO but also keeps your
supporters informed about your campaign's
progress. Schedule regular updates, whether
it's announcing a new policy position,
sharing details about upcoming events, or
highlighting successful fundraising efforts.
Consistency in updating the website
demonstrates your campaign's activity and
commitment.

Finally, it's crucial to test your website's
functionality thoroughly. Before launching
your website, ensure all links work correctly,
forms submit data appropriately, and the
website is user-friendly across different
devices and browsers. Seek feedback from
trusted
individuals to identify any issues or areas for
improvement. A well-tested website avoids
technical glitches and presents a professional
image to your audience.

Remember, your campaign website is more
than just a static
collection of information. It's a dynamic tool
that can be leveraged to

connect with voters, build support, and ultimately, secure victory.

Invest the time and resources necessary to create a professional, engaging, and effective website that works to support your campaign goals. By following the steps outlined above, you can build a

powerful online presence that helps you reach more voters and make your campaign a resounding success.

Mastering Social Media for Political Campaigns

Building a robust online presence extends far beyond simply having a well-designed website. In today's hyper-connected world, mastering social media is non-negotiable for any successful political campaign. Social media platforms offer unparalleled opportunities to connect directly with voters, bypass traditional media gatekeepers, and build grassroots support in ways unimaginable just a few decades ago. However, simply having accounts on various platforms is
insufficient; a strategic and consistent approach is crucial to maximize impact and achieve campaign goals.

Facebook, with its vast user base and robust targeting capabilities, remains a cornerstone of modern political campaigning. Effective Facebook strategies involve more than just posting campaign updates. Consider utilizing Facebook's advertising platform to target specific demographics based on age, location, interests, and even voting history. This allows for highly efficient allocation of resources, ensuring your message reaches the most receptive

audiences. Run A/B tests on different ad creatives to optimize your return on investment. Don't underestimate the power of visually appealing content – high-quality photos and videos are significantly more engaging than text-only posts. Consider live streams of rallies, town halls, or Q&A sessions to create an authentic connection with potential voters. Facebook groups can be used to cultivate

communities of support, fostering engagement and encouraging organic sharing of campaign materials.

Beyond paid advertising, organic engagement is equally important on Facebook. Regularly posting engaging content, such as behind-the-scenes glimpses of your campaign activities, personal stories that connect with voters on an emotional level, and responses to relevant news events, will help build a loyal following and increase brand awareness. Monitor your Facebook analytics closely to understand what type of content resonates most with your audience, and adapt your strategy accordingly. Engage directly with comments and messages, responding thoughtfully and promptly. This shows voters that you're actively listening and that you value their input.

Twitter, with its short-form messaging and real-time updates, is ideal for quickly disseminating information, responding to breaking news, and engaging in public discourse. Use relevant hashtags to increase the visibility of your tweets. Develop a consistent brand voice and tone that reflects your personality and campaign message. Don't be afraid to use humor and wit where appropriate, but always maintain a professional and respectful demeanor. Engage with other users, particularly influencers and journalists, to expand your reach and build relationships. Twitter's trending topics can offer valuable insights into what's on voters' minds, allowing you to tailor your messaging accordingly. Pay attention to the tone of your tweets; a single poorly-worded tweet can have significant repercussions.
Consider creating separate Twitter accounts for your campaign and your personal profile, to maintain a clear separation between your professional and personal brand.

Instagram, a visually-driven platform, offers a powerful opportunity to create a more personal connection with voters. High-quality photography and videography are paramount; this is where showcasing your personality and campaign values becomes crucial. Use Instagram Stories to share behind-the-scenes content, Q&As, and polls to increase engagement. Employ Instagram's features, such as reels and carousels, to present information in a dynamic and appealing format. Collaborate with local influencers to expand your reach and credibility. While less effective for direct fundraising compared to Facebook, Instagram plays a significant role in building brand affinity and creating a positive impression among voters.

Beyond these three major platforms, consider expanding your presence to other networks based on your target audience's preferences and your campaign's specific needs. TikTok, for example, can be exceptionally effective for reaching younger voters, particularly through creative and engaging short videos. LinkedIn, a more professional platform, can be useful for connecting with business leaders and influencers. However, spreading your resources too thinly across too many platforms may dilute your impact. Focus on the platforms where your target demographic is most active, and prioritize quality over quantity.

Remember that consistency is key to success on all social media platforms. Develop a content calendar to ensure regular posting of engaging material. Schedule posts in advance to maintain a consistent online presence, even when you're busy with other campaign activities. Don't be afraid to experiment with different types of content, formats and posting times to find what works best for your specific audience and campaign. Monitor your analytics regularly and adjust your strategy based on the data, as this is the only way to see tangible results. This might entail experimenting with different posting times, altering the types of content being posted, or revising the targeting of your paid ad campaigns. Constantly evaluate your progress and refine your approach accordingly.

Crucially, maintain a consistent brand identity across all your social media platforms. Use the same logo, color palette, and tone of voice to create a cohesive brand image. Link all your social media profiles to your campaign website to drive traffic and consolidate your online presence. This reinforces brand recognition and simplifies navigation for voters who want to learn more about your campaign.

Furthermore, actively respond to comments and messages on all your social media platforms. Engage in respectful dialogue, even with those who disagree with your views. This demonstrates your willingness to listen and engage in a civil discourse, which can be a valuable asset in building a positive image and cultivating trust with your audience.

Social media presents both opportunities and challenges. Negative comments and online attacks are inevitable. Have a plan in place to address these issues promptly and professionally. Assign a member of your campaign team to monitor social media and respond to critical comments and issues. Avoid getting drawn into unproductive arguments, focusing instead on highlighting positive aspects of your campaign.

Finally, don't neglect the human element. Social media is a tool for connection, not just broadcasting. Use it to showcase your personality and values, building genuine relationships with voters.

Authenticity resonates far more effectively than carefully-crafted slogans and polished images. Let your passion for your cause shine through, building a campaign that inspires engagement, participation, and ultimately, electoral success.

Leveraging Email Marketing for Voter Engagement

Building a strong online presence requires a multi-pronged approach, and while social media plays a vital role, email marketing remains a powerful, often underestimated tool for voter engagement. It allows for direct, personalized communication, fostering a deeper
connection with supporters than fleeting social media posts can often achieve. Think of email as your personal, direct line to your voters, a way to cultivate relationships and build a loyal base of supporters long before election day arrives.

The cornerstone of successful email marketing lies in building a robust and targeted email list. This isn't about collecting as many addresses as possible; it's about acquiring high-quality leads – individuals who have demonstrated genuine interest in your campaign and its platform. Avoid purchasing email lists; these are often filled with invalid or uninterested recipients, leading to poor deliverability rates and harming your sender reputation. Instead, focus on organic list building through various avenues.

Your website should prominently feature an email signup form. Make it easy to find, visually appealing, and clearly communicate the benefits of subscribing. Offer incentives, such as exclusive content, early access to campaign updates, or invitations to special events.
Consider offering different signup options based on levels of
engagement. For example, you could have one form for receiving general updates, another for volunteer opportunities, and a third for major fundraising announcements. This allows subscribers to choose the level of communication they prefer, reducing unsubscribes and maintaining a highly engaged audience.

Integrate signup forms into your social media presence. On
Facebook, you can use lead generation ads that directly capture email addresses, while on other platforms, you can link to your website's signup form in your bio and incorporate it into your posts. At campaign events, rallies, and meet-and-greets, actively encourage attendees to sign up for your email list. Have signup sheets

available, and even consider using tablets or
laptops to facilitate online signup.

Make it a fun, engaging process, maybe offering a small giveaway to those who sign up on the spot.

Always be transparent about how you will use the email addresses you collect. In your signup form, clearly state what types of emails subscribers will receive and how frequently. This builds trust and helps manage expectations. Complying with data protection
regulations like GDPR and CAN-SPAM is critical. These regulations outline
requirements for email marketing, including obtaining
explicit consent, providing an easy unsubscribe option, and
accurately identifying yourself as the sender. Neglecting these
regulations can result in hefty fines and damage your campaign's reputation irreparably.

Once you have a list, crafting compelling email campaigns becomes crucial. Avoid generic, mass-produced emails. Personalization is key to improving engagement. Use the recipient's name, if possible, and tailor the content to their

specific interests and location whenever feasible. Segment your list based on demographics, prior engagement levels (e.g., donors vs. volunteers), or expressed policy preferences.
This allows you to send targeted messages that resonate with each segment.

The subject line is your first impression. It needs to be captivating and compelling enough to encourage recipients to open your email.
A/B testing different subject lines can significantly improve open rates.
Experiment with various approaches: using a question,
highlighting a benefit, creating a sense of urgency, or personalizing the subject line based on the recipient's name or location. Keep them concise and avoid spam triggers like excessive capitalization or exclamation points.

The email body should be clear, concise, and visually appealing. Use high-quality images and videos to enhance engagement. Don't overwhelm the reader with walls of text. Break up the content into short paragraphs with bullet points and subheadings to improve readability. Always include a clear call to action (CTA). What do you want the recipient to do after reading the email?

Donate? Volunteer? Attend an event? Make the CTA prominent and easy to find.

Include strong visuals. People respond to
visual stimuli. Use high-quality
photographs and videos that capture the
energy and
excitement of your campaign. Consider
showcasing relatable
moments with constituents – a friendly
conversation, a meeting with a local
business owner, or a visit to a community
center. This adds a human element, making
your campaign more approachable and
trustworthy.

Regular email communication is vital.
Consistent engagement keeps your campaign
top-of-mind, but don't bombard your
subscribers with emails. Find a balance that
keeps them informed without
overwhelming them. Consider a weekly or
bi-weekly newsletter with updates on your
campaign's progress, upcoming events, and
important policy announcements. Use email
to share personal stories and anecdotes to
connect with voters on an emotional level.
Share photos and videos from campaign
events and interactions with the community.

Monitor your email metrics closely. Track open rates, click-through rates, and unsubscribe rates to assess the effectiveness of your campaigns. Use analytics to identify what works and what doesn't. Analyze which subject lines perform best, which calls to action are most effective, and which segments are most responsive. Use this data to refine your strategy and improve future campaigns.

Don't neglect mobile optimization. Many people open emails on their smartphones. Ensure your emails are responsive and display
correctly on various devices. Use concise text, clear calls to action, and large, easily clickable buttons.

Email marketing automation tools can streamline your efforts. These platforms allow you to schedule emails, personalize content, and track results. Many offer features like A/B testing, segmentation, and automated email sequences based on subscriber behavior. They can be a huge time-saver, allowing you to focus on other aspects of your campaign.

Finally, always comply with all
relevant laws and regulations
regarding email marketing. Respect
your subscribers' privacy.
Provide a clear and easy-to-use unsubscribe
mechanism, and avoid sending unsolicited
emails. Remember, building trust with your
email subscribers is essential for long-term
success. A well-executed email marketing
strategy can be a significant asset in building
a loyal base of supporters and ultimately
winning the election. Treat each email as an
opportunity to build a relationship, not just
deliver a message. The more personalized
and authentic your approach, the more
effective your email campaigns will be.

Utilizing Online Fundraising Platforms

Building a robust online presence extends beyond email marketing and social media engagement; it necessitates a sophisticated online fundraising strategy. This is where platforms like WinRed and Anedot come into play, offering powerful tools to harness the potential of online donations. These platforms aren't merely donation portals; they are integral components of a comprehensive digital fundraising ecosystem, demanding a strategic approach to maximize their effectiveness.

WinRed, frequently favored by Republican candidates and organizations, provides a user-friendly interface designed for ease of use, even for those unfamiliar with online fundraising intricacies. Its strength lies in its seamless integration with various other campaign tools and technologies, streamlining the entire fundraising process.
One key advantage is its ability to process recurring donations effectively. This

feature is crucial for establishing a steady stream of funding, ensuring financial stability throughout the campaign. Regular, recurring donations provide predictability in cash flow, allowing for better budget management and strategic resource
allocation. Instead of relying on sporadic large donations, a campaign using WinRed can cultivate a base of smaller, consistent contributions, fostering a more sustainable financial foundation.

Beyond recurring donations, WinRed offers robust reporting and analytics capabilities. Understanding donor demographics, donation patterns, and campaign performance metrics is vital for making informed decisions. The platform provides detailed reports, offering insights into donor behavior and preferences. This information allows for targeted fundraising strategies, enabling the campaign to focus its efforts on the most responsive segments of the donor pool. For example, by identifying the most successful donation appeals, the campaign can replicate successful strategies and refine less successful ones. Analyzing donation patterns can reveal the most effective times to solicit donations, optimizing outreach and
maximizing return on investment (ROI).

However, success with WinRed, or any online fundraising platform, requires more than simply setting up an account. The platform itself is just a tool; the effectiveness lies in the strategic deployment of its features. Compelling call-to-action messages are paramount. The language used in donation requests must resonate with potential donors, conveying the urgency and importance of the campaign. A poorly worded appeal can deter potential donors, whereas a persuasive and empathetic message can significantly increase donation rates. This requires careful crafting of messaging, thoroughly testing different approaches to identify the most effective appeals. A/B testing different versions of donation appeals, subject lines, and website copy allows campaigns to refine their messaging and optimize their conversion rates. Continuous monitoring and adjustment of these factors are essential for sustained success.

Anedot, while also a robust platform, often appeals to a broader range of political campaigns, including those with smaller budgets or limited technical expertise. Its user-friendly interface simplifies the process of setting up and managing fundraising campaigns. While it may lack some of the advanced features offered by larger platforms like WinRed, its ease of use and affordability makes it an attractive option for many candidates. Anedot offers features designed to make managing multiple fundraising appeals relatively effortless. The ability to track donations across different appeals, combined with detailed reporting features, allows for informed decision-making regarding future fundraising efforts.

Anedot's strengths lie in its flexibility and adaptability. It offers customizable options, allowing campaigns to tailor the platform to their specific needs. This is crucial, as every campaign is unique and requires a tailored approach. For example, a local campaign might require different messaging and fundraising strategies compared to a national campaign. Anedot's ability to accommodate these
differences makes it a versatile tool adaptable to different campaign scenarios. Furthermore, Anedot provides excellent customer support, assisting users with technical issues and providing guidance on best practices. For less tech-savvy campaigns, this support is invaluable,

ensuring a smooth and efficient fundraising process.

However, both WinRed and Anedot require a strategic approach beyond simply creating an account and posting a donation button.

Effective use of these platforms necessitates a comprehensive understanding of online fundraising best practices. This includes crafting compelling donation appeals, targeting the right audiences, and employing effective email marketing strategies to promote the fundraising efforts. Integration with social media is also vital; linking the fundraising platform to the campaign's social media profiles increases visibility and reach, driving traffic to the donation page. This synergistic approach leverages the power of multiple channels to maximize fundraising potential.

Furthermore, transparency and trust are paramount. Potential donors need to feel confident that their donations are being used responsibly and effectively. Clearly outlining how the funds will be used, providing regular updates on campaign progress, and maintaining transparency in financial reporting builds trust and encourages repeat donations. This can be achieved through regular email updates to donors, showcasing the impact of their contributions. It's not enough to simply request donations; showcasing how those donations are making a tangible difference significantly increases the likelihood of securing further support.

Optimizing the donation process is equally critical. A seamless and user-friendly donation process is crucial to prevent potential donors from abandoning their donation attempts due to frustration or technical difficulties. This necessitates carefully designing the
donation page, minimizing the number of steps required to complete a donation. The use of secure payment gateways, clear instructions, and multiple payment options enhance the user experience and increase conversion rates. Testing different donation processes can pinpoint bottlenecks and identify areas for improvement, leading to a more efficient and user-friendly system.

Beyond technical aspects, cultivating a strong donor relationship is crucial for long-term success. This involves thanking donors for their contributions, providing regular updates on campaign progress, and fostering a sense of community among supporters. This can involve creating exclusive content for donors, offering opportunities for

interaction with the candidate, or
organizing virtual events to engage
supporters. This personalized touch
transcends mere transactional interactions,
cultivating a deeper connection with
donors,
encouraging repeat contributions and
advocacy.

Finally, it's vital to remember that
compliance with all relevant campaign
finance regulations is non-negotiable.
Accurately
recording and reporting all donations is
crucial to maintaining
transparency and avoiding legal
complications. Understanding and adhering
to the specific rules and regulations
governing online fundraising practices is not
merely a matter of compliance; it is essential
for preserving the credibility and integrity of
the campaign. A failure to comply with these
regulations can have serious legal and
reputational consequences, potentially
jeopardizing the entire
campaign. Regularly reviewing and updating
the campaign's
understanding of these regulations is
essential to ensure continued compliance.

The effective utilization of online fundraising platforms like WinRed and Anedot requires a multi-faceted approach. It's not merely about choosing a platform; it's about strategically integrating it into a broader digital fundraising strategy, encompassing compelling messaging, effective email marketing, transparent communication, and unwavering adherence to legal regulations. Success lies in cultivating a relationship with donors, providing value, and demonstrating the impact of their contributions. Through a meticulous and comprehensive approach, candidates can leverage these platforms to build a strong financial foundation, crucial for a successful and impactful campaign.

Online Advertising Strategies for Political Campaigns

Building upon a strong online fundraising foundation, the next crucial element of a successful digital campaign is a well-defined online advertising strategy. This involves more than simply placing ads; it requires a nuanced understanding of various platforms, precise audience targeting, and rigorous performance measurement. Ignoring this aspect is akin to navigating a vast ocean without a map – you might reach your destination eventually, but the journey will be unnecessarily arduous and far less efficient.

The first step is platform selection. While platforms like Facebook, Instagram, Google Ads, and Twitter are widely used, the optimal choice depends heavily on your target demographic and campaign message. A candidate targeting younger voters might find Instagram and TikTok particularly effective, leveraging visually engaging content and short-form videos to maximize reach. However, a candidate focusing on older voters might find more success on Facebook, where demographic targeting options are more mature and user engagement often centers around longer-form content and news articles.

Google Ads, while seemingly broad, offers powerful tools for granular targeting based on keywords, demographics, location, and even interests. Imagine a campaign focusing on environmental policy. Google Ads allows you to target users who frequently search for terms like "climate change," "renewable energy," or "environmental protection." This targeted approach ensures that your message reaches individuals actively interested in the issues at the heart of your campaign. This precise targeting minimizes wasted ad spend and maximizes the return on investment (ROI).

Once you've chosen your platforms, the next critical step is crafting compelling ad creatives. This isn't simply about creating visually appealing images or videos; it's about conveying your core message concisely and persuasively. Remember, your ad copy is your first impression – make it count. Keep it brief, focused, and memorable.

Use strong calls to action, urging viewers
to visit your website, sign up for email
updates, or make a donation.

A/B testing is essential. Create multiple
versions of your ads, varying the imagery,
headline, and call to action, and track their
performance.
This data-driven approach allows you to
identify which creatives resonate most
with your target audience, enabling you
to optimize your campaigns for
maximum impact. Neglecting A/B
testing is a missed opportunity to refine
your messaging and improve your
campaign's efficiency.

Targeting your audience precisely is equally
crucial. Online
advertising platforms provide sophisticated
targeting options,
allowing you to reach specific demographic
groups, geographical areas, and even
interest-based segments. For example, you
can target voters based on their age, income,
education level, political
affiliation, and online behavior. This laser-
focus minimizes wasted ad spend and
maximizes the likelihood of converting

impressions into valuable engagement –
website visits, donations, volunteer sign-ups,
or votes.

Beyond demographic targeting, consider
psychographic targeting.
This involves segmenting your audience
based on their values, beliefs, and
lifestyles. If your campaign platform
emphasizes family values, you can target
users who frequently engage with family-
oriented content online. Similarly, if you're
advocating for
environmental protection, you can target
users who show an interest in
environmental causes or sustainability.

Once your campaigns are running,
monitoring their performance is paramount.
Regularly analyze key metrics such as click-
through rates (CTR), conversion rates, cost
per click (CPC), and cost per
acquisition (CPA). These metrics provide
valuable insights into the effectiveness of
your campaigns and allow you to make data-
driven adjustments to improve their
performance. For instance, if your CTR is
consistently low, you might need to revise
your ad creatives or refine your targeting
parameters.

Budget allocation is another critical aspect of online advertising. It's essential to allocate your budget strategically across different
platforms and campaigns based on their performance and ROI. Don't pour all your resources into a single platform or campaign without first testing and analyzing the results. A well-diversified approach, combined with data-driven adjustments, maximizes the return on your investment. Consider using a campaign management platform that allows for easy tracking and budgeting across various platforms.

Legal compliance is also critical. Familiarize yourself with relevant advertising regulations, ensuring your campaigns adhere to all
applicable laws and guidelines. False or misleading statements can have severe consequences, damaging your reputation and potentially leading to legal repercussions. Maintaining transparency and honesty in your advertising is paramount. Transparency fosters trust with voters, which is crucial for a successful campaign.

Beyond paid advertising, consider organic reach. This involves actively engaging with your audience on social media platforms, sharing relevant content, and fostering two-way communication.
Organic engagement complements your paid advertising efforts, building brand awareness and reinforcing your campaign's message. The synergy between paid and organic efforts is often more impactful than either alone.

Finally, remember that online advertising is not a one-size-fits-all solution. The optimal strategy will depend on your specific campaign goals, target audience, and available resources. Continuous experimentation, data analysis, and adaptation are essential for optimizing your campaigns and maximizing their impact. Regularly review your performance, identify areas for improvement, and iterate your strategy based on the data you collect.

This continuous cycle of analysis, adaptation, and optimization is the key to running successful online advertising campaigns. Treat it as an ongoing process, not a one-time event. Embrace the iterative nature of digital marketing and use data to inform your decisions. By continuously refining your approach, you will significantly improve your campaign's reach, engagement, and ultimately, its success.

Consider the example of a local mayoral race. The candidate might utilize Facebook to target residents within specific neighborhoods based on age and interests. Simultaneously, they could run Google Ads campaigns targeting individuals searching for local news or community events. By combining these strategies and meticulously analyzing the performance of each, the candidate can optimize their spending and maximize their reach.

Another example could involve a statewide senatorial campaign. The candidate might use a combination of Facebook, Instagram, and Twitter, employing visually appealing content on Instagram and concise, impactful messaging on Twitter. Google Ads could target voters based on their political affiliations and search history. Consistent monitoring and optimization of these various channels are key to a successful campaign.

Ultimately, successful online advertising in political campaigns demands a strategic approach. It requires a blend of creative ad design, precise audience targeting, rigorous

performance tracking, and a deep
understanding of the nuances of different online
platforms. By mastering these elements, candidates can significantly enhance their campaign's reach, engagement, and ultimately, their chances of electoral success. The investment in this strategic approach will yield significant returns, leading to a more efficient and impactful campaign. Remember, in the digital age, an effective online presence isn't just beneficial; it's essential.

Identifying and Cultivating HighValue Donors

Identifying and cultivating high-value donors is crucial for the financial success of any political campaign. These individuals, often possessing significant wealth and influence, can provide substantial financial support, enabling broader outreach and more effective campaigning. The process, however, requires a strategic and nuanced approach, combining meticulous research, personalized communication, and consistent engagement.

The first step involves creating a comprehensive donor database. This database shouldn't just be a list of names and contact information; it should be a detailed profile of each potential donor, including their political affiliations, past donation history (if available through public records), professional background, philanthropic interests, and any known connections to the campaign or its

principles. Information gleaned from social media, news articles, and professional networking sites can be invaluable in creating a well-rounded picture of each prospective donor. This level of detail allows for targeted outreach, ensuring that each
communication is relevant and resonates with the individual's
personal values and interests. Tools like DonorSearch or similar platforms can significantly aid in gathering this information
efficiently and ethically.

Once a database of potential high-value donors has been compiled, the next stage involves developing a structured outreach strategy.
This is not a "one-size-fits-all" approach. High-value donors are often busy individuals, requiring a personalized and respectful approach. Initial contact might involve a handwritten note from the candidate expressing genuine appreciation for their potential contribution and outlining the campaign's core mission and goals.
This personal touch demonstrates respect for the donor's time and underscores the campaign's sincerity. Follow-up communications should be strategically timed and tailored to specific events or

milestones in the campaign, such as the launch of a new fundraising initiative or the release of a policy paper. It's crucial to avoid overwhelming donors with excessive communication; quality over quantity is paramount.

The quality of the communication itself is also paramount. High-value donors are not merely seeking an opportunity to write a check; they are investing in a cause they believe in. Therefore,
communication should focus on the impact of their contribution –how their support will translate into tangible results, such as increased voter outreach, improved advertising campaigns, or the expansion of community engagement efforts. Use data and metrics to illustrate the effectiveness of the campaign's strategy and highlight the potential return on investment for their contribution. For
example, you might present data showing the impact of previous campaign fundraising efforts on voter turnout or media coverage. The goal is to establish a clear link between the donor's contribution and the achievement of the campaign's objectives.

Cultivating relationships with high-value donors is an ongoing process, extending beyond the fundraising phase. Regular

updates on campaign progress, invitations to exclusive events (such as private briefings with the candidate or smaller fundraising gatherings), and personalized thank-you notes are all essential for maintaining positive engagement. It's vital to remember that these individuals are not merely sources of funding; they are stakeholders in the campaign's success, and their ongoing support is essential. Consider creating a dedicated team to nurture these relationships, ensuring consistent and personalized communication throughout the campaign and beyond. This team should be comprised of individuals with strong interpersonal skills and a deep understanding of donor
motivations.

Furthermore, it's essential to demonstrate transparency and
accountability in the management of campaign funds. High-value donors expect a clear understanding of how their contributions are being used. Regular financial reports, outlining income and expenditure, and detailing the progress of key campaign initiatives, foster trust and enhance donor confidence. This level of transparency can be particularly important in addressing any concerns or questions the donor may have. Providing opportunities for donors to interact

with the campaign team and ask
questions directly can further
solidify these relationships.

Beyond individual donors, exploring
opportunities for partnerships with relevant
organizations or corporations is also
beneficial. These partnerships can not only
bring in financial resources but also expand
the campaign's reach and influence.
However, any such partnerships should be
carefully considered and vetted to ensure
alignment with the campaign's values and
principles. Transparency and disclosure are
essential in these partnerships as well,
avoiding any potential conflicts of interest.

Another important aspect is identifying potential "influencer"
donors.
These are individuals who may not have
the financial capacity to make large
donations themselves but have significant
influence within their networks. Engaging
these individuals can lead to
referrals and introductions to other
potential high-value donors. It's a form of
"viral" fundraising, harnessing the power
of social influence to expand the
campaign's financial base.

Finally, ethical considerations must always be at the forefront of any fundraising strategy. Transparency, accountability, and respect for donor privacy are not just good practice; they are essential for maintaining trust and integrity. Campaign finance laws and
regulations must be strictly adhered to, and any potential conflicts of interest must be carefully managed and disclosed. Maintaining ethical standards not only safeguards the campaign's reputation but also strengthens the long-term relationship with donors, ensuring their continued support in future endeavors.

The cultivation of high-value donors is a complex yet rewarding endeavor, requiring a multifaceted approach that blends research, personalized communication, and transparent accountability. By carefully crafting a strategy that respects donor time and values, and by consistently demonstrating the impact of their contributions, campaigns can secure the financial resources necessary to achieve their objectives. The long-term investment in these relationships often pays dividends beyond the immediate campaign cycle, establishing a base of support for future electoral efforts and

reinforcing the candidate's position within their
political ecosystem.
The payoff from building these valuable
connections often extends well beyond the
immediate campaign, establishing a network
of support for future endeavors and
strengthening the candidate's
political standing. A well-cultivated network
of high-value donors can transform a
campaign's viability, ensuring resources are
available to effectively compete and achieve
victory.

Crafting Compelling Donor Prospectuses

Crafting a compelling donor prospectus is akin to crafting a compelling narrative—a story that resonates with the potential donor's values and aspirations. It's not simply a request for money; it's an invitation to partnership, a chance to be part of something bigger than themselves. To achieve this, the prospectus must go beyond a dry recitation of financial needs; it must paint a vivid picture of the campaign's vision, its impact, and the role the donor will play in its success.

The first crucial step is understanding your target audience. High-net-worth individuals are not a monolithic group. Their motivations for donating vary widely – some are driven by ideological alignment, others by a desire for community impact, and still others by a combination of factors including tax benefits and social prestige. Thorough research is essential to identify the specific interests and priorities of each potential donor. This research extends beyond publicly available information. You need to understand their philanthropic history, their involvement in other organizations, and their stated values. This level of detail allows for a highly personalized approach, significantly increasing the likelihood of a positive response.

Once you've segmented your potential donor base, you can begin tailoring your prospectuses. A generic appeal will likely fall flat; a personalized approach, however, demonstrates respect for the donor's time and intelligence. This personalization should extend to every aspect of the prospectus, from the salutation to the call to action. The language used should reflect the donor's preferred style of communication, avoiding jargon and overly technical terms.
Consider the donor's preferred method of communication as well; some may prefer a formal letter, while others might respond better to a concise email or a personal phone call.

The structure of the prospectus itself is vital. It should follow a clear and logical narrative arc, leading the reader from an understanding of the problem to the proposed solution and finally to a clear call to

action. Begin by outlining the campaign's
core mission and goals in concise and
engaging language. Avoid overly technical
political jargon; instead, focus on the
human impact of the campaign's work.
Use compelling storytelling techniques to bring the
issue to life.
Paint a picture of the challenges faced
by your constituents, and emphasize
the transformative power of your
campaign.

Next, articulate the specific problem your
campaign addresses. Clearly define the issue
and its consequences if left unaddressed. Use
data and statistics to support your claims, but
present this information in a visually
appealing and easily digestible manner.
Charts, graphs, and infographics can be
incredibly effective in conveying complex
information in a concise and compelling
way. Avoid overwhelming the reader with
too much data; focus on the most relevant
and
impactful information.

Then, detail the campaign's strategy for addressing
the problem.

Clearly outline your proposed solutions, and explain how your campaign plans to implement them. Be realistic and transparent; avoid making unrealistic promises or exaggerating your capabilities. Emphasize the campaign's unique approach and its potential for achieving tangible results. This is where you can demonstrate the expertise and experience of your team, building confidence in the campaign's ability to deliver on its promises.

Following the strategic overview, emphasize the impact of the donor's contribution. Clearly articulate how their investment will help to achieve the campaign's goals. Quantify the impact whenever possible; for example, "Your contribution of $10,000 will enable us to reach 10,000 voters through direct mail," or "A $5,000 donation will allow us to run targeted digital ads in key demographics." Show donors the tangible results their money will create, emphasizing the positive impact on the community. This demonstrates accountability and transparency, building trust and encouraging future contributions.

Finally, include a clear and concise call to action. Make it easy for donors to

contribute, providing multiple options for
giving, such as online donations, checks,
or wire transfers. Include all relevant

contact information, including a phone number and email address.
Consider offering various donation levels with corresponding benefits, such as invitations to exclusive events or recognition in campaign materials. This creates a sense of value and encourages higher levels of giving.

Beyond the written prospectus, consider supplementary materials. A short video showcasing the candidate's vision and the campaign's impact can be a powerful tool. This allows potential donors to connect with the candidate on a personal level, building trust and rapport. High-quality photography and compelling visuals can also enhance the overall appeal of the prospectus. Ensure all materials are professionally designed and reflect the campaign's branding and messaging.

Remember, the donor prospectus is not a one-size-fits-all document.
It requires a nuanced understanding of your target audience and a skillful ability to tailor the message to resonate with their individual values and motivations. Regular follow-up is also critical. After sending the prospectus,

follow up with a personal phone call or email to address any questions and further cultivate the relationship.
Building strong relationships with high-value donors is an ongoing process that requires consistent engagement and appreciation.
Ultimately, the success of your fundraising efforts depends not only on the quality of your prospectuses but also on the strength of the relationships you build with your donors.

The creation of a compelling donor prospectus is a multifaceted process that extends beyond simply outlining financial needs. It involves a deep understanding of your potential donors, a well-crafted narrative that resonates with their values, and a commitment to transparency and accountability. By crafting persuasive materials that effectively communicate the campaign's vision, impact, and the role donors will play in its success, campaigns can secure the
financial resources necessary to achieve their goals and ultimately, win the election. This process requires meticulous attention to detail, a clear understanding of your target audience, and the ability to tell a compelling story that resonates with potential donors on a personal level. It is an

investment in building long-term
relationships that can

benefit the campaign far beyond the current election cycle. The result of this thoughtful and strategic approach is not simply financial support but the creation of a network of engaged and passionate supporters who are invested in the campaign's success. The ongoing nurturing of these relationships through regular communication, consistent updates, and transparent accountability will further solidify the foundation of your campaign's financial stability and ensure its long-term sustainability. Think of it as a strategic partnership, where the donor's investment translates into tangible, positive change, and their contribution is not merely a transaction but a meaningful act of collaboration towards a shared goal.

Organizing Successful Fundraising Events

Building upon the foundation of a compelling donor prospectus, the next crucial step in securing the financial resources necessary for a successful campaign involves organizing and executing effective fundraising events. These events serve as vital opportunities to cultivate relationships with potential donors, solidify existing support, and generate significant revenue. However, a successful fundraising event requires meticulous planning and execution, extending far beyond simply sending out invitations.

The first step is identifying the appropriate type of event. The choice should align with the campaign's overall strategy, target audience, and available resources. A high-profile gala dinner might attract significant donations from wealthy individuals and corporations, but it requires substantial investment in venue rental, catering, and entertainment. Conversely, a more intimate coffee meet-and-greet offers a less expensive, more personal setting to connect with a wider range of donors, fostering grassroots support. Smaller, localized events, such as town hall meetings with a fundraising component, can effectively target specific demographics and build community engagement. The key is to select an event format that best suits the campaign's goals and resources.

Regardless of the chosen format, a detailed budget is paramount. This budget should encompass all potential costs, including but not limited to venue rental, catering, decorations, entertainment, marketing and advertising, staffing, and any potential unforeseen expenses. A thorough cost analysis allows for realistic fundraising goals and prevents financial setbacks. This budget should be developed alongside a realistic fundraising projection based on the number of expected attendees, potential donation amounts, and anticipated sponsorship levels. This dual approach—budgeting and projection—ensures a financially sound approach to the event planning.

Effective marketing and promotion are essential to maximize attendance. A comprehensive marketing strategy should leverage a multi-channel approach, encompassing both traditional and digital mediums. This might involve designing and distributing eye-catching flyers and brochures, utilizing email marketing campaigns, harnessing the power of social media platforms like Facebook, Twitter, and Instagram to spread the word, and potentially utilizing paid advertising on these platforms to extend the reach. Strategic partnerships with local media outlets can also garner significant publicity and increase event awareness. The key is to create a buzz around the event, piquing the interest of potential attendees and donors. A clear, concise event webpage with online registration should complement these efforts, streamlining the registration process and maximizing attendance.

The selection of a suitable venue plays a crucial role in the event's success. The venue should align with the planned event format and projected attendance. It should be accessible to attendees, providing adequate parking or public transportation options. The atmosphere of the venue should also be considered – a formal setting might be appropriate for a gala, while a more casual atmosphere might be more suitable for a meet-and-greet. Beyond the physical space, the venue should offer necessary amenities such as catering facilities, audio-visual equipment, and adequate space for registration and networking. Securing the venue well in advance is critical, especially for popular locations, ensuring availability on the chosen date.

Creating a compelling event program is essential to engage attendees.
The program should be meticulously planned, ensuring a smooth flow of events and maximizing audience engagement. This involves crafting a balanced program that effectively integrates fundraising elements with compelling content, such as presentations by the candidate, testimonials from supporters, or entertainment to keep the audience engaged and enthusiastic. The program should also incorporate opportunities for networking and interaction between the candidate and potential donors, fostering a sense of community and shared purpose.

On the day of the event, seamless execution is critical. A well-trained volunteer team is essential to handle registration, manage logistics, and ensure the smooth operation of the event. The volunteer team should be adequately briefed on their roles and responsibilities, ensuring everyone understands their contribution to the overall success of the event. Contingency plans should be developed to address potential unforeseen issues, such as technical malfunctions or unexpected changes in attendance. This preparedness demonstrates professionalism and ensures the event proceeds smoothly, even amidst challenges.

Post-event follow-up is as important as the event itself. Thank-you notes should be promptly sent to attendees and donors, expressing gratitude for their support and reiterating the campaign's mission and goals. This post-event communication reinforces the relationship with donors and cultivates long-term support. A detailed accounting of the event's financial performance should also be documented, analyzing the successes and areas for improvement to inform future fundraising efforts. The data gathered— attendance figures, donation amounts, sponsorship levels, feedback—provides invaluable insights to refine future strategies and maximize the effectiveness of future events.

Beyond the logistics and execution, the success of a fundraising event hinges on the creation of an atmosphere of warmth, engagement, and shared purpose. This requires careful attention to detail, from the welcoming ambiance to the tone of the messaging. It's crucial to create a connection between the campaign's goals and the donors' values. This emotional connection transcends a mere transaction, transforming the contribution into an act of investment in a shared vision. This feeling of shared purpose and mutual investment can significantly improve fundraising success, laying the foundation for lasting relationships and sustained financial support for the campaign.

The effectiveness of fundraising events can be further enhanced through strategic partnerships and sponsorships. Seeking sponsorships from local businesses or organizations can significantly offset event costs and increase overall revenue. In return for their sponsorship, businesses can be offered various levels of recognition, including prominent placement of their logos on event materials, speaking opportunities, or special mentions during the event. This mutually beneficial arrangement generates additional resources for the campaign while providing businesses with valuable brand exposure. Selecting sponsors who align with the campaign's values and target audience is paramount; misaligned sponsorships can negatively impact the campaign's image and reputation.

Leveraging technology to enhance the fundraising experience is crucial in today's digital landscape. Online registration platforms simplify the process for attendees, allowing for easy registration and payment processing. Live-streaming the event for those unable to attend in person can expand the reach and engagement. Integrating mobile payment options allows for seamless transactions during the event. Utilizing digital tools for donor management and follow-up ensures effective communication and relationship building with supporters. This comprehensive digital approach not only streamlines the logistics of the event but also maximizes the reach and impact of the fundraising efforts.

The ultimate goal of organizing successful fundraising events is not simply to raise money, but to build a strong network of engaged supporters who are invested in the campaign's success. This involves nurturing relationships, fostering a sense of community, and demonstrating transparency and accountability in the use of funds.

By consistently communicating with donors, providing regular updates on campaign progress, and publicly acknowledging their contributions, the campaign cultivates trust and loyalty. This strategic approach to fundraising creates a sustainable ecosystem of support that benefits the campaign far beyond the immediate fundraising event. It's about building relationships, cultivating trust, and inspiring ongoing commitment, ensuring the long-term financial health and success of the campaign. This commitment to relationship-building is the cornerstone of a sustainable and thriving fundraising strategy.

Managing Campaign Finances and Reporting

Building on the successful execution of fundraising events and the cultivation of donor relationships, the next critical phase of a
campaign's financial strategy involves meticulous management of the funds raised and strict adherence to all financial reporting requirements. This aspect, often overlooked in the excitement of securing contributions, is crucial for maintaining transparency, ensuring legal compliance, and building public trust—all vital
components of a successful campaign. Effective financial
management is not merely about balancing the books; it's about demonstrating fiscal responsibility, showcasing the campaign's commitment to ethical practices, and fostering confidence among donors and the public.

The first step in managing campaign finances effectively is
establishing a robust accounting system.

This goes beyond simply tracking income and expenses. A comprehensive system should categorize each transaction, clearly identifying its source and
purpose. Software specifically designed for campaign finance
management can greatly simplify this process, offering features like automated expense tracking, reconciliation tools, and reporting capabilities that adhere to regulatory standards. Many platforms offer integration with banking systems, further streamlining the process.
Maintaining detailed records of every donation received, including the donor's name, address, occupation, and the amount contributed, is paramount. This information is not only vital for accurate reporting but also for cultivating donor relationships and ensuring compliance with campaign finance laws.

Regular reconciliation of bank statements with the campaign's
accounting records is essential. This process identifies any
discrepancies and allows for immediate correction, preventing
potential errors from escalating.
Discrepancies, no matter how small, should be investigated thoroughly and documented. This diligence demonstrates a commitment to financial accuracy and transparency,

which builds trust with donors and the public. Furthermore, regular reviews of the campaign's budget, comparing actual spending against projected expenses, are essential for identifying potential financial challenges and making necessary adjustments. This proactive approach to budget management ensures that the campaign remains financially viable throughout the election cycle.

Beyond the internal management of funds, navigating the complexities of campaign finance regulations is a critical aspect of this stage. Depending on the jurisdiction, campaigns may be required to file regular reports with relevant election authorities, disclosing all contributions and expenses. The frequency of these reports, the level of detail required, and the specific reporting forms vary significantly depending on the laws governing the election. Failure to comply with these reporting requirements can result in significant penalties, including fines and even campaign disqualifications. Therefore, familiarizing oneself with the relevant regulations early in the campaign process is essential. Consulting with legal counsel specializing in campaign finance law is highly recommended,

particularly for navigating complex
regulations and ensuring full compliance.

Understanding the different categories of
campaign contributions is also crucial.
Many jurisdictions distinguish between
individual contributions, political action
committee (PAC) contributions, and other
types of funding. Each category may have
different
contribution limits and reporting
requirements. For example,
individual contributions often have lower
limits than PAC
contributions, and specific disclosure
requirements might apply to contributions
from certain entities or individuals.
Thorough
understanding of these regulations will
prevent accidental violations and
demonstrate the campaign's commitment to
ethical and legal conduct.

The use of technology in managing
campaign finances is not merely a
convenience; it's a necessity for efficiency
and compliance.
Software designed for campaign finance
management can automate many tasks,
reducing the risk of human error and
freeing up
campaign staff to focus on other critical
aspects of the campaign. Features like

automated donation processing, expense tracking, and report generation can save significant time and resources.

Furthermore, secure online platforms for managing donations ensure the safety and confidentiality of donor information, enhancing trust and transparency.

In addition to effective financial management practices, establishing clear financial controls and internal checks and balances are equally crucial. This requires designating specific individuals responsible for different aspects of financial management, establishing authorization processes for all expenditures, and implementing procedures for reviewing and approving all financial transactions. This layered approach minimizes the risk of fraud or errors, reinforcing the campaign's commitment to ethical and accountable financial practices.

The importance of transparency in campaign finance cannot be overstated. Publicly sharing financial information, such as contribution reports and expenditure summaries, not only demonstrates accountability but also builds trust with donors and voters. This

transparency strengthens the campaign's credibility and fosters public confidence in its operations. Making financial information readily available online or through easily accessible reports allows voters to scrutinize the campaign's spending,
enhancing transparency and fostering trust.

Furthermore, consistent communication with donors regarding the use of their contributions is vital. Regular updates, newsletters, or even short videos explaining how funds are being allocated can strengthen donor relationships and reinforce their commitment to the campaign. This communication should not only outline the specific ways funds are being used but also showcase the tangible results and progress being made with their contributions. This demonstrates the campaign's responsible use of funds, building trust and potentially encouraging future contributions.

Finally, understanding and complying with post-election financial requirements is also crucial. Many jurisdictions have specific regulations regarding the disposition of remaining campaign funds after the election is concluded. These regulations may dictate how leftover funds can be used, whether they can be transferred to other

political entities, or whether they must be returned to donors. Failure to comply with these post-election requirements can result in

penalties and investigations. Therefore, proactively understanding and following these regulations is as vital as adhering to pre-election financial requirements. A detailed plan for the disposition of remaining funds should be developed well in advance of the election to ensure a smooth and compliant transition. This forward-thinking approach demonstrates meticulous planning and commitment to financial integrity, leaving a positive and lasting impression on donors and the public. In conclusion, effective management of campaign finances is not merely a logistical detail; it is a fundamental element of running a successful and ethical political campaign.

Diversifying Your Fundraising Sources

Diversifying your fundraising strategy is paramount to building a robust and sustainable financial foundation for your campaign. Relying solely on individual donors, however generous, exposes your campaign to unpredictable fluctuations and potential shortfalls. A well-rounded approach involves cultivating a diverse portfolio of funding sources, mitigating risk and maximizing your fundraising potential. This requires a strategic and multifaceted approach, going beyond the traditional methods to tap into a wider range of potential contributors.

One critical area to explore is the realm of small-dollar donations.
These contributions, while individually modest, can collectively represent a significant source of funding, particularly when harnessed through effective online fundraising strategies. Platforms like ActBlue and WinRed, tailored specifically for political campaigns, provide user-friendly interfaces that simplify the donation

process for potential contributors. These platforms often integrate seamlessly with social media and email marketing, enabling campaigns to reach broader audiences and encourage recurring donations. Furthermore, highlighting the impact of even small contributions—emphasizing how a collective of small donations can achieve substantial campaign goals—can significantly boost participation and engagement.

Success in small-dollar fundraising often hinges on building a strong online presence, crafting compelling narratives that resonate with potential donors, and utilizing data analytics to target specific demographics with personalized messaging. Regular email updates, social media engagement, and compelling campaign videos can all contribute to building a culture of small-dollar support.

Beyond individual donors, corporate sponsorships offer another valuable avenue for campaign funding. However, navigating this terrain requires sensitivity and a clear understanding of ethical considerations and potential conflicts of interest. Transparency is paramount. Any sponsorship received should be publicly disclosed, ensuring accountability and building trust with voters. The nature of the sponsorship should be carefully considered, avoiding any

arrangements that could compromise the campaign's independence or create the appearance of undue influence. For instance, accepting sponsorship from a corporation with a vested interest in a policy area central to the campaign's platform might raise ethical concerns.

Therefore, seeking sponsorships from companies whose interests align broadly with your campaign's overall goals, rather than specific policy positions, is a more prudent approach. Strategically aligning with organizations that share your campaign's values, such as

environmental groups supporting a candidate focused on climate change, can be a more ethical and impactful method.

Political Action Committees (PACs) represent another significant source of campaign funding. PACs are organizations established to raise and spend money to elect and defeat candidates. They can represent various interests, from labor unions and industry groups to ideological organizations. Developing relationships with relevant PACs aligned with your campaign's platform is crucial. This involves actively engaging with their representatives,

highlighting the
campaign's core values and objectives, and demonstrating how your candidacy aligns with their interests. A well-crafted proposal outlining the campaign's strategy, its potential impact, and its
alignment with the PAC's goals can significantly enhance your chances of securing funding. Attending PAC events, engaging in direct communication with their leadership, and demonstrating a deep understanding of their priorities are all effective ways to
cultivate these relationships. However, it's imperative to maintain transparency regarding PAC contributions, clearly disclosing their support in accordance with all relevant legal and ethical guidelines.

In addition to these established avenues, exploring more innovative fundraising strategies can significantly broaden your financial reach. Crowdfunding platforms, while often associated with entrepreneurial ventures, can be effectively leveraged for political campaigns.
Platforms like Kickstarter or GoFundMe can be utilized to raise smaller donations from a larger pool of supporters, particularly if the campaign has a compelling story and a strong online presence. This requires a well-crafted campaign narrative, strong social media engagement, and effective marketing

to reach potential donors across various platforms. A visually appealing crowdfunding page, emphasizing the campaign's objectives and the impact of contributions, is essential.

Another relatively untapped area is the pursuit of grants from foundations and non-profit organizations. Many foundations actively support political causes aligned with their missions. Identifying foundations whose areas of focus align with your campaign's platform is critical. This requires thorough research to identify potential funders and preparing detailed grant proposals that articulate the campaign's objectives, its alignment with the foundation's mission, and its expected outcomes. A well-researched and meticulously crafted grant proposal that clearly demonstrates a connection between your campaign's goals and the foundation's philanthropic priorities is crucial for securing funding.

Furthermore, hosting fundraising events that go beyond the traditional dinner or cocktail party format can significantly enhance participation and fundraising success. Organizing themed events tailored to your target demographics—for example, a family-friendly picnic for a candidate focused on children's issues or a sporting event for a candidate interested in promoting athletic programs—can make fundraising more engaging and appeal to a wider range of supporters. These events require careful planning, including securing a suitable venue, managing logistics, and creating a compelling atmosphere.

The careful design of the event, a vibrant social media campaign promoting it, and the involvement of influential community members can significantly influence attendance and increase the potential for fundraising success.

Finally, maximizing your campaign's fundraising potential requires effective data management. Tracking donations, maintaining donor records, and utilizing data analytics to identify potential donors are all critical components of a successful fundraising strategy. Investing in a robust campaign management system, capable of tracking donations and managing donor communications efficiently, is a wise investment. This system should provide clear reports on fundraising progress, donor demographics, and contribution patterns, which are invaluable for refining your fundraising strategies over time. Data analysis enables you to identify high-potential donors, tailor your fundraising appeals to specific demographics, and optimize your outreach efforts. By integrating data collection, analysis, and donor management, you can improve the efficiency and effectiveness of your fundraising activities.

In conclusion, diversification of fundraising strategies is not merely a matter of increasing your campaign's financial resources; it is about building a resilient and sustainable financial foundation, capable of weathering unexpected challenges and sustaining a strong and effective campaign. By actively exploring and implementing a comprehensive approach—that encompasses small-dollar donations, corporate sponsorships, PAC contributions, innovative fundraising techniques, grant applications, and diligent data management—you can maximize your fundraising potential and build the resources necessary for a successful and impactful campaign. The key lies in a multifaceted strategy, combined with meticulous planning, transparency, and a deep understanding of ethical considerations. Remember, a campaign's financial stability is directly correlated with its success, and a well-diversified fundraising strategy is the cornerstone of a financially secure and ultimately, victorious campaign.

Defining Your Core Campaign Message

Crafting a winning campaign message is arguably the most critical aspect of any successful political campaign. It's the bedrock upon which all other strategies—fundraising, volunteer recruitment, media outreach—are built. Without a clear, resonant message, even the most meticulously planned campaign can falter. This message must not only define the candidate but also resonate deeply with the target audience, effectively communicating their vision, values, and proposed solutions to the electorate's concerns. It's the heart of your campaign, the narrative that connects with voters on an emotional level and motivates them to support your cause.

Defining your core message requires a deep understanding of your candidate, their strengths, weaknesses, and overall political philosophy. This process is not simply about summarizing policy positions; it's about distilling the essence of the candidate's personality, their motivations, and their

unique approach to the issues at hand.
Consider what genuinely sets your candidate apart. What unique experiences or perspectives do they bring to the table? What are their core values, and how do those values translate into concrete policy proposals? These questions are crucial to shaping a message that is both authentic and persuasive.

Begin by conducting thorough research into your candidate's background. Examine their professional career, community involvement, personal life, and any significant achievements or challenges they have overcome. This background research will unearth anecdotes, experiences, and principles that can be woven into a compelling narrative. Focus on identifying key moments and experiences that reveal the candidate's character, values, and commitment to public service. This is not just about compiling facts; it's about finding the stories that truly capture the essence of who they are and why they are running for office.

Next, you need to delve into the specifics of your target audience.
Understanding your target voters' demographics, concerns, and aspirations is

paramount in crafting a message that will resonate with

them. Avoid generic statements; tailor your message to address the specific needs and anxieties of your target demographic. For instance, a message emphasizing economic opportunity might resonate strongly with working-class voters, while a message focusing on environmental protection might be more effective with younger, environmentally conscious voters. Utilize polling data, focus groups, and other research methods to gain a comprehensive understanding of your target audience's priorities and concerns. This will inform not only the content of your message but also the tone and style of your communication.

Once you have a deep understanding of your candidate and your target audience, you can begin to articulate your core message. This message should be concise, memorable, and easily understood. Avoid complex jargon or overly technical language. The ideal message should be simple enough to be conveyed in a soundbite, yet nuanced enough to capture the complexities of your candidate's platform. Think of it as a carefully constructed elevator pitch –concise, impactful, and immediately memorable. This succinct message should be your guiding principle, informing all aspects of your campaign, from your website and social media posts to your campaign literature and public speeches.

A powerful campaign message often employs a compelling narrative. Instead of simply listing policy proposals, weave these proposals into a larger story about the candidate's vision for the future. This narrative should explain why the candidate is running, what problems they aim to solve, and how their vision will benefit the electorate. The narrative should evoke emotions and create a sense of hope and possibility. Consider the classic narrative arc—a beginning, a conflict, and a resolution—and apply it to your campaign message. Show the voters what the current situation is, the problems with the status quo, and how your candidate's plan offers a solution and a better future.

Remember to maintain consistency throughout your message. Your messaging should align across all platforms and communications. Any inconsistencies will create confusion and undermine the credibility of your campaign. Ensure that every communication reinforces the core message, conveying a unified and consistent narrative. This requires meticulous planning and coordination across your entire campaign team.

Furthermore, testing and refinement are critical steps in the process. Continuously monitor the public's reaction to your message through polls, focus groups, and social media engagement. Be prepared to adapt and refine your message based on this feedback. A rigid, inflexible message is unlikely to resonate with the evolving needs and preferences of the electorate.

Another crucial aspect is differentiating your message from your opponents'. Thoroughly analyze your opponents' platforms and messages. Identify their strengths and weaknesses. What are the key points of disagreement, and how can you highlight your candidate's superior approach? Craft your message to emphasize your candidate's unique strengths and address any weaknesses effectively. Avoid direct attacks; instead, focus on highlighting your candidate's positive attributes and

contrasting them with your opponents'
shortcomings. A positive message that
focuses on solutions is
generally more effective than a negative
message that focuses on attacks.

Finally, keep the message human. Avoid
sterile political rhetoric. Instead, use
relatable language, personal anecdotes, and
imagery that connect with voters on an
emotional level. Remember, the ultimate
goal is to build a connection between your
candidate and the voters.
This connection transcends policy positions
and delves into the shared values,
aspirations, and concerns that bind a
community together. By emphasizing these
shared experiences and showing empathy
for the voters' struggles, you can forge a
deeper connection and strengthen your
campaign's appeal.

In summary, crafting a winning campaign
message is a multifaceted process that
requires careful planning, meticulous
research, and constant adaptation. By
understanding your candidate, identifying
your target audience, articulating a clear and
concise core message, and developing a
compelling narrative, you can create a
message that resonates deeply with voters
and lays the foundation for a successful

campaign. Remember that the message is not merely a set of talking points, but a living, breathing narrative that evolves and adapts alongside the campaign itself. A message that is authentic, relatable, and consistently reinforced across all channels will ultimately prove more effective in winning over voters and securing victory.

Identifying Your Target Voters

Understanding your electorate isn't about simply knowing the demographics; it's about deeply understanding their lived experiences, their aspirations, and their anxieties. This involves going beyond surface-level statistics and delving into the nuances of their concerns. A successful campaign doesn't just target voters; it connects with them on a human level. This section will explore the strategies to effectively identify and understand your target voters, turning data into actionable insights that shape your message and campaign strategy.

The first step is data collection. This involves more than just pulling numbers from voter registration databases. While those databases provide valuable information on age, registration status, and party affiliation, they don't tell the whole story. You need to supplement this data with qualitative research to gain a deeper understanding.

Consider employing various methods to gain a holistic picture of your target voter groups. Publicly available census data can provide valuable insights into demographic trends within your district or state. Pay close attention to income levels, educational attainment, racial and ethnic composition, and age distribution. This will offer a broad overview to segment your electorate. However, this alone is insufficient.

Next, turn to more targeted research methods. Conduct focus groups, bringing together small groups of representative voters from different segments to discuss their concerns, priorities, and voting habits. These conversations, facilitated by experienced moderators, can reveal hidden anxieties and aspirations that may not be evident in surveys. Observe their body language, listen to the nuances of their responses, and actively probe for deeper explanations. Don't just ask what issues are important to them; ask
why
they're important.
Understanding the underlying motivations behind their opinions is crucial to crafting a message that resonates.

Surveys offer a broader reach than focus groups but require careful design to avoid skewed results. Develop clear, concise questions that avoid leading language or jargon. Pre-test your survey instrument on a small sample group to identify any ambiguities or areas for improvement. Online surveys can provide a cost-effective method of gathering data from a larger pool of respondents, but ensure your sample accurately reflects the demographic distribution of your electorate to avoid bias. Consider using weighting techniques to adjust for any discrepancies in the sample.

Beyond surveys and focus groups, consider conducting one-on-one interviews. These in-depth conversations allow for more nuanced exploration of individual voter perspectives. These interviews should be structured yet flexible, allowing for follow-up questions that delve deeper into the voter's reasoning and experiences. Remember to actively listen; the goal isn't to convince them, but to understand their point of view.

Analyzing social media can also yield valuable insights. Monitor relevant hashtags, join online forums and groups frequented by your target voters, and pay attention to the conversations taking place. What issues are they discussing? What are their concerns? What language do they use? Social media provides a rich source of qualitative data that can supplement your quantitative findings. However, remember to approach social media analysis critically; online communities can be echo chambers, and the views expressed may not always accurately reflect the broader electorate.

Finally, don't underestimate the power of direct engagement.
Organize meet-and-greets, town halls, and community events to directly interact with potential voters. Listen to their questions, concerns, and stories. These interactions provide invaluable insights into the pulse of the community and allow you to humanize your candidate and build personal connections. This grassroots interaction can reveal information that's impossible to glean from surveys or focus groups.

Once you've gathered data from multiple sources, it's time for analysis. Consolidate your findings, looking for patterns and common themes across different data sets. Identify key issues that resonate across various segments of your target audience, as well as areas of potential disagreement or division. Creating detailed voter personas can be helpful. These are fictional representations of ideal voters within each segment, outlining their demographics, values, concerns, and media consumption habits. These personas should be based on your research findings and will help you focus your messaging efforts.

For example, let's consider a hypothetical campaign targeting
suburban swing voters. Initial demographic data might reveal a relatively high level of income and education, with a mix of party affiliations. Further research—focus groups, surveys, and social media analysis—might reveal concerns about property taxes, school quality, and local infrastructure. One-on-one interviews might uncover anxieties about the changing demographics of their
community and a desire for stability and predictability. By analyzing this data, you can craft a message that speaks directly to these

concerns, highlighting your candidate's commitment to responsible fiscal policies, improved education, and community development.

Another example: A campaign targeting younger voters might
discover, through social media analysis and focus groups, that
climate change and affordable healthcare are paramount. Further investigation reveals concerns about student debt and a desire for meaningful political engagement. This understanding informs a messaging strategy that directly addresses these issues, emphasizing your candidate's commitment to environmental protection, accessible healthcare, and student loan reform. This personalization of the message is critical.

By combining quantitative data (demographics, registration statistics) with qualitative research (focus groups, interviews, social media analysis), you gain a comprehensive understanding of your target voters. Remember, the goal is not simply to identify who your voters are, but to understand their perspectives, motivations, and concerns. This deep understanding allows you to craft a message that resonates deeply, building trust, fostering connection, and ultimately, winning their votes. This detailed, multi-faceted approach to voter

identification is crucial for the success of any political campaign. It moves beyond simply checking boxes on a demographic sheet and into the realm of truly understanding the human beings you're trying to reach. The result is a campaign that is not just strategically sound, but genuinely connects with the electorate on an emotional and intellectual level. Ignoring this crucial step is a recipe for disaster. Understanding your voters is not just a strategy; it's the foundation upon which a winning campaign is built. Invest the time and
resources in this phase; the payoff will be substantial.

Developing a Persuasive Narrative

Building a persuasive narrative isn't about listing policy positions; it's about weaving a compelling story that resonates with voters on an emotional level. Your candidate isn't just a collection of policy proposals; they're a person with a unique background, experiences, and motivations. This section focuses on transforming your candidate and their platform into a narrative that captivates and inspires.

The first step is identifying the core narrative. What is the central theme that unites your candidate's vision, their background, and their proposed policies? This isn't just a slogan; it's a comprehensive story that explains
why
your candidate is running,
what
they hope to
achieve, and
how
they plan to get there. For example, a candidate might frame their narrative around

"restoring the American Dream," "building a stronger community," or "securing a brighter future for our children." This central theme should be clear, concise, and easily understood. It should be the unifying thread that ties all aspects of the campaign together.

Once the core narrative is established, it needs to be woven into every aspect of the campaign. This requires a consistent and cohesive message across all communication channels. Your website, social media posts, campaign literature, speeches, and even your candidate's interactions with voters should all reinforce this central theme. Inconsistency undermines credibility and confuses voters. Imagine a candidate running on a platform of fiscal responsibility while simultaneously proposing expensive, unfunded programs. The resulting dissonance will damage the candidate's trustworthiness and ultimately harm their chances of success.

Crafting a compelling narrative requires understanding the art of storytelling. This involves more than just presenting facts and figures; it requires connecting with voters on an emotional level. Effective storytelling uses vivid language, compelling imagery, and relatable anecdotes to draw voters in and make them feel a personal connection to the candidate and their vision. This emotional connection is crucial for driving voter engagement and securing their support. Consider using personal stories from the candidate's life to illustrate key points and build empathy. For instance, a candidate who overcame adversity might share their personal journey to inspire hope and demonstrate resilience. Similarly, a candidate might use stories of constituents they've helped to illustrate the impact of their work and demonstrate their commitment to serving the community.

Remember, your narrative should also address potential criticisms.
Anticipate likely attacks from opponents and develop counter-narratives to address those concerns head-on. This proactive approach prevents opponents from defining the narrative and allows you to control the flow of information. Don't shy away from difficult topics; address them directly and honestly. Transparency builds trust, and a well-crafted response to criticism can actually strengthen your campaign's message. A candidate facing accusations of financial impropriety, for example, might proactively release their tax returns and explain any potentially suspicious transactions to preempt damaging attacks and maintain transparency.

Beyond the candidate's personal narrative, you must also craft a compelling story around their policy positions. Avoid dry recitation of policy details; instead, translate complex issues into relatable stories that demonstrate the real-world impact of your candidate's proposals. For example, rather than simply stating a plan to improve infrastructure, you could tell the story of a local family whose commute is drastically impacted by a dilapidated bridge and showcase how the candidate's plan directly addresses this issue. This approach makes the policy relevant and emotionally resonant, transforming it from an abstract concept into a tangible benefit for the community.

Visual storytelling is also crucial. Use compelling images, videos, and graphics to create a memorable and engaging experience for voters. Visuals have a powerful impact on shaping perceptions and emotions, effectively complementing and enhancing your narrative. A photograph of the candidate volunteering at a local soup kitchen, for example, conveys a sense of community engagement and compassion far more powerfully than a written description.
Furthermore, consider the use of short, impactful videos to convey

complex policy proposals in an easily digestible format. These videos should use compelling visuals and engaging narratives to convey the candidate's vision and resonate emotionally with voters.

The development of a persuasive narrative is an iterative process. It's not a one-time effort but rather an ongoing refinement and adaptation based on feedback from voters, polling data, and analysis of the political landscape. Throughout the campaign, continuously monitor the effectiveness of your narrative and make adjustments as needed.
Utilize focus groups and surveys to assess how your message is being received and identify areas for improvement. Be prepared to adapt your messaging based on emerging issues and changing voter sentiment. A successful campaign isn't static; it adapts and evolves to remain relevant and resonate with the evolving needs and priorities of the electorate.

Don't underestimate the power of authenticity. Voters are discerning and can quickly spot inauthenticity. Ensure that the narrative you create aligns with the

candidate's genuine values and beliefs. An artificial or manufactured image will quickly unravel, eroding trust and harming the campaign. Authenticity fosters genuine connection with voters, building credibility and strengthening the campaign's message. It is vital that your campaign's messaging remains
consistent across all channels. Inconsistency creates confusion and undermines trust. Everything from social media posts to campaign flyers should reinforce your central message.

Finally, consider using storytelling techniques that resonate with the particular cultural context of your target audience. Familiar
storytelling tropes, local legends, or historical references can create a sense of shared identity and build stronger connections.
Understanding the cultural landscape is as important as
understanding the demographics, ensuring that your message isn't just heard but truly understood and embraced.

By mastering these techniques, you can transform your candidate and their platform into a compelling narrative that captures the hearts and minds of voters, significantly increasing their chances of electoral success. Remember that the narrative isn't just a communication tool;

it's the heart of your campaign, guiding
every decision and
interaction, from policy choices to
campaign strategy and media appearances.
Building a strong, consistent, and authentic
narrative is the cornerstone of a successful
political campaign.

Messaging for Different Media Channels

The core message—the central narrative you've painstakingly crafted—is the bedrock of your campaign. But its effectiveness hinges on its adaptability. A message that resonates on Twitter might fall flat on a television screen, and a compelling radio spot might be lost in the noise of a crowded social media feed. Therefore, tailoring your message to each medium is crucial. This isn't about changing the core message, but rather, adjusting its delivery to maximize impact across diverse platforms.

Let's start with social media. Social media demands brevity and visual appeal. Think short, impactful videos showcasing the candidate's personality and key policy positions. Use strong visuals –images and short video clips are far more effective than walls of text. Consider the platform's specific nuances: Instagram favors visually striking content; Twitter thrives on concise, punchy statements; Facebook allows for longer posts but necessitates engaging visuals and questions to encourage interaction. On these platforms, your message should be conversational, engaging, and relatable. Avoid overly formal language; aim for a tone that's authentic and approachable. Use relevant hashtags to expand your reach and engage with trending topics related to your campaign's themes.

Remember, social media is a two-way street. Active engagement with comments and direct messages is paramount. Responding promptly and thoughtfully demonstrates responsiveness and strengthens your connection with voters. Consider running targeted advertising campaigns on platforms like Facebook and Instagram to reach specific demographic groups with tailored messaging.

Print media offers a different opportunity. While reaching a potentially smaller audience than social media, print provides a level of permanence and authority that digital platforms often lack. Newspapers, brochures, and flyers allow for more detailed explanations of your candidate's platform. Use high-quality design and compelling visuals to grab the reader's attention. Your messaging should be clear, concise, and well-structured, using bullet points and

concise sentences to highlight key
arguments. Consider using

testimonials from respected community members or endorsements from influential figures to build credibility. For example, a local newspaper advertisement could feature a large, compelling
photograph of the candidate alongside a concise summary of their key policy planks, perhaps focusing on a particularly pressing local issue. In a brochure, you might offer a more in-depth explanation of their policy positions, supplemented with supporting data and personal anecdotes. Remember to always include clear contact information, encouraging readers to engage further with the
campaign.

Television offers a unique challenge and opportunity. Television advertisements need to be impactful and memorable in a very short time. A 30-second spot demands a highly focused message, typically a single powerful idea or image. This means carefully selecting compelling visuals and soundbites that convey the essence of your candidate and their vision. You'll need to work closely with a
professional videographer and editor to produce a visually appealing and

emotionally resonant advertisement.
Consider using upbeat music and positive imagery to create a feeling of optimism and hope.
Remember that television viewers are easily distracted, so your message needs to be immediate and engaging from the very first second. Test various versions of your ad to determine which resonate best with your target audience. Pre-testing your ads with focus groups can provide invaluable insight into their effectiveness.
Consider using A/B testing on social media to refine your message before committing to expensive television advertising.

Radio provides a different platform for message delivery. While lacking the visual element of television, radio relies on strong storytelling and memorable soundbites. The audio experience needs to be engaging and dynamic, using music and sound effects to create an immersive listening experience. This might mean focusing on the candidate's personal story, their experiences, or a powerful anecdote that underscores their campaign platform. Consider using a professional voice-over artist to add professionalism and impact to your message. Your message should be memorable, using repetition and strong imagery to reinforce key points. Consider a series of radio ads, each focusing on a different aspect of the candidate's platform, to maximize impact.

Beyond these major media channels, consider the power of direct mail. While often overlooked in the digital age, targeted direct mail can be surprisingly effective, particularly with older demographic groups. High-quality, visually appealing postcards or flyers can deliver your message directly to voters' homes, providing a tangible and memorable reminder of your candidate. A well-designed direct mail piece can include a compelling image, a concise message, and a clear call to action, like visiting your campaign website or attending a town hall meeting. The key to effective direct mail is personalization and targeting – ensuring your message reaches the right voters at the right time.

In summary, the challenge lies not in altering the core message, but in understanding how to shape its delivery for maximum impact across different channels. Each platform has its own unique characteristics and audience, and your messaging strategy must be tailored

accordingly. Through strategic planning, thoughtful design, and rigorous testing, you can ensure your candidate's message resonates powerfully across all media, ultimately maximizing their chances of electoral success. Remember, consistent messaging is crucial. While the style and format may vary across platforms, the underlying narrative and core values must remain consistent,
ensuring a unified and impactful campaign. This unified approach ensures that the voter, regardless of the media channel they engage with, receives a clear and consistent message, strengthening their overall impression and increasing the likelihood of their support. Careful planning and rigorous testing are essential elements in the development of a multifaceted and effective media strategy.

Responding to Opponent Attacks

Responding to opponent attacks is an inevitable aspect of any political campaign. Ignoring them is rarely a viable strategy; silence can often be interpreted as weakness or tacit admission of guilt. However, reacting impulsively or defensively can be equally damaging. The key lies in developing a proactive and strategic communication plan that anticipates potential attacks and crafts effective counter-measures. This plan must be multifaceted, employing various communication channels and addressing the attacks with a blend of factual refutation, strategic deflection, and positive messaging.

The first step in crafting a robust response strategy is thorough research and anticipation. Your campaign team should meticulously monitor your opponent's statements, social media activity, and public appearances for potential vulnerabilities or areas of attack. This involves not just listening to what they say, but also understanding their underlying motivations and target audience. Are they trying to appeal to a specific demographic? Are they highlighting a particular issue to mobilize a specific voter base? Understanding their strategy allows you to anticipate their attacks and prepare targeted responses.

Once potential attack points are identified, the next step is to develop a comprehensive response plan. This isn't simply a list of talking points; it's a detailed strategy outlining how to address each potential attack across multiple platforms. For instance, a false claim made in a televised debate requires a different response than a negative advertisement circulating on social media. A televised debate demands a swift, concise, and impactful rebuttal delivered directly to the audience. Social media requires a more nuanced approach, possibly including a fact-check, a video response, or even a preemptive strike highlighting the opponent's inconsistencies.

For example, if an opponent accuses your candidate of lacking experience in a particular policy area, your response shouldn't be a simple denial. Instead, you could proactively highlight the candidate's related experience, perhaps emphasizing their work on similar issues at the local level, their involvement in relevant organizations, or endorsements from experts in that field. You could release a policy paper detailing their detailed stance on the issue, demonstrating a thorough understanding that surpasses the opponent's superficial critique. This proactive approach shifts the narrative from a perceived weakness to a strength.

In crafting your responses, clarity and accuracy are paramount. Avoid overly technical jargon or overly complex explanations; stick to simple, easily digestible information. Ensure that all claims are backed by credible sources, whether it's statistical data, expert opinions, or documented evidence. Using verifiable facts not only strengthens your argument but also undermines the credibility of the opponent's attacks. When dealing with false accusations, it's crucial to debunk them directly and clearly, using the facts to expose the misinformation. This directly addresses the attack, while simultaneously demonstrating your commitment to transparency and truthfulness.

Furthermore, it's vital to consider the emotional response your
response will evoke. While factual accuracy is critical, it's equally important to convey empathy and understanding. Acknowledge the concerns raised by the opponent, even if you disagree with their conclusions. This demonstrates that you're listening and that you take the concerns of voters seriously, fostering a sense of connection and trust. By acknowledging concerns while delivering a clear refutation, you can diffuse tension and demonstrate leadership.

Another effective strategy is to redirect the conversation toward your positive message. Instead of solely focusing on refuting negative attacks, use them as an opportunity to reiterate your core campaign themes and values. This involves strategically linking the opponent's attacks to your own policy proposals or campaign promises. For example, if an opponent criticizes your candidate's stance on
education, you can use this as an opportunity to highlight your detailed education plan, emphasizing its benefits to families and communities. This approach shifts the focus away from the negative attack and towards the positive aspects of your campaign.

Moreover, remember that your response is not just about addressing the attack itself, but also about shaping public perception of both you and your opponent. Consider the overall tone and style of your response. Maintaining a professional and respectful approach, even when facing aggressive attacks, can be highly effective. Responding with anger or personal attacks often backfires, giving the opponent an opportunity to paint you as unhinged or petty. Conversely, a calm, measured, and professional response demonstrates maturity and leadership qualities, ultimately enhancing your image in the eyes of the voters.

Finally, it's crucial to utilize a multi-pronged communication strategy.
Don't rely solely on press releases or social media posts. Engage traditional media outlets like television and radio to get your message across to a broader audience. Consider organizing press conferences to directly address major attacks. Utilize your grassroots network to help disseminate your responses and engage in direct conversations with voters. And most importantly, prepare your candidate for these types of attacks.

Role-playing and mock debates can help them anticipate potential lines of attack and develop strong, confident responses.

In conclusion, effectively responding to opponent attacks is not about winning a verbal sparring match; it's about shaping public perception and reinforcing your campaign's core message. By proactively anticipating attacks, developing a multifaceted response strategy, and using each attack as an opportunity to reiterate your positive
message, you can successfully navigate the challenges of a political campaign and emerge stronger. Remember, the goal is not to merely defend against attacks but to use them to showcase the strength, integrity, and competence of your candidate. A well-crafted response strategy isn't merely reactive; it's a dynamic tool that reinforces your campaign's narrative and strengthens your connection with the
voters. By combining factual accuracy with emotional intelligence and strategic communication, you can transform what might seem like a crisis into an opportunity to demonstrate your candidate's fitness for office.

Building a Strong Volunteer Base

Building a robust volunteer base is the bedrock of any successful grassroots campaign. Volunteers provide the manpower essential for canvassing, phone banking, event organization, and countless other crucial tasks. Without a dedicated team of volunteers, even the best-funded campaigns struggle to reach their full potential. This section details the strategies for recruiting, training, motivating, and managing a highly effective volunteer force.

The first step in building a strong volunteer base is identifying
potential volunteers. Don't limit yourself to your immediate circle of friends and family. Tap into your existing networks – professional organizations, community groups, religious institutions, and social clubs – to identify individuals who share your campaign's values and are willing to contribute their time and energy. Utilize your campaign website and social media platforms to reach a broader audience. Make

it easy for people to sign up online, providing clear instructions and different volunteer options to cater to various time commitments and skill sets. Consider creating a dedicated volunteer signup page on your website, using a simple form to capture essential information such as name, contact details, available time, and preferred volunteer activities.

Once you've identified potential volunteers, the next crucial step is to effectively recruit them. Your recruitment efforts should go beyond a simple request for help. Clearly articulate your campaign's mission, values, and goals, emphasizing the impact volunteers will have on achieving those goals. Highlight the positive aspects of volunteering– the chance to make a difference, meet new people, and gain valuable experience in political campaigning. Focus on the personal connection and sense of community volunteering offers. Share compelling stories of past volunteer successes, emphasizing the tangible results of volunteer efforts.

Training your volunteers is essential for ensuring efficiency and effectiveness. A well-trained volunteer is a productive volunteer. Organize comprehensive training sessions, covering the basics of

campaign organization, voter outreach techniques, phone banking protocols, canvassing strategies, data entry procedures, and any other relevant skills needed for the specific tasks. Provide clear guidelines and scripts for volunteers to follow, ensuring consistency in
messaging and approach. Make the training sessions engaging and interactive, using real-life examples and role-playing exercises to enhance learning. Consider breaking down the training into smaller, manageable modules, allowing volunteers to attend based on their availability and preferred roles. Utilize a combination of online and in-person training methods, providing flexibility and catering to different learning styles.

Keeping your volunteers motivated is equally important. Regular communication is key to maintaining morale and enthusiasm.
Regular updates on campaign progress, volunteer accomplishments, and upcoming events are crucial. Offer opportunities for recognition and appreciation. Organize volunteer appreciation events, highlighting their contributions and

showing gratitude for their hard work. Publicly acknowledge volunteers' efforts through social media posts, newsletters, or even simple thank-you notes. Celebrate milestones and successes together, reinforcing the sense of shared purpose and accomplishment. Consider creating a dedicated
volunteer appreciation program, rewarding volunteers for their consistent contributions with special recognition or small gifts.

Effective volunteer management is critical to maximizing their contributions. Assign clear roles and responsibilities to each volunteer, ensuring everyone understands their specific tasks and how they contribute to the overall campaign goals. Provide regular feedback and support, addressing concerns promptly and offering guidance as needed. Use volunteer management software to track volunteer hours, tasks, and progress, ensuring efficient organization and coordination. This software can also help with communication, scheduling, and task assignments, simplifying the management process and allowing for a more efficient workflow. Regularly check in with volunteers to assess their needs, address any challenges, and ensure they feel valued and supported.

Beyond the core tasks, consider diversifying volunteer roles. Offer opportunities for individuals with specialized skills to contribute their expertise. This could involve graphic designers, website developers, social media managers, data analysts, or legal professionals who can assist in various aspects of the campaign. Having a diverse volunteer base with varying skills allows the campaign to leverage their
collective strengths, leading to a more efficient and effective
campaign.

Finally, remember that your volunteers are your ambassadors. They are the face of your campaign in the community, and their interactions with voters can make or break your efforts. Ensure that your volunteers are well-informed about your campaign's platform, values, and goals. Equip them with the necessary tools and resources to effectively communicate your message to potential voters. Their enthusiasm and passion for your cause will be contagious, and they will play a vital role in building support for your campaign. By investing in your volunteers, you invest in the success of your campaign. A well-trained, motivated, and well-managed volunteer base is the foundation upon which a successful grassroots campaign is built. Their dedication and hard work will directly translate into increased voter engagement, broader outreach, and ultimately, a stronger chance of electoral victory.

Effective Canvassing Strategies

Effective canvassing is more than just knocking on doors; it's about building genuine connections with voters. It's about understanding their concerns, addressing their doubts, and ultimately, inspiring them to support your campaign. A well-executed canvassing strategy can significantly boost voter turnout and shift the electoral landscape in your favor. This requires meticulous planning, a highly motivated team, and a deep understanding of your target audience.

First, you need a comprehensive voter database. This isn't just a list of names and addresses; it's a detailed profile of each voter. Ideally, your database should include information like age, party affiliation, voting history, and key interests. This data allows you to tailor your canvassing approach to resonate with specific groups of voters. For instance, you might focus on environmental issues when canvassing in a neighborhood known for its environmental activism, or emphasize economic concerns in areas

struggling with
unemployment. This targeted approach
maximizes your impact and avoids wasting
valuable time on ineffective strategies. Tools
like voter file software can significantly
enhance the effectiveness of your database
management. These programs allow you to
segment your voter lists, track canvassing
progress, and analyze the effectiveness of
your outreach efforts.

Next, you need to train your volunteers
rigorously. Simply handing them a script and
sending them out into the field is a recipe for
disaster. Your volunteers need to be well-
versed in your campaign's platform, able to
answer tough questions with confidence, and
skilled at engaging voters in meaningful
conversations. Role-playing
exercises can be invaluable in this process.
Simulate various
scenarios, from enthusiastic supporters to
staunch opponents, and equip your
volunteers with the skills to handle each
situation
effectively. Beyond the technical aspects of
the campaign, emphasize the importance of
active listening and respectful
communication. Every interaction should be
an opportunity to build trust and rapport,
regardless of the voter's initial stance. A
friendly, approachable demeanor can go a
long way in influencing undecided voters.

Beyond the training, consider equipping your volunteers with the right tools. Provide them with high-quality maps, clearly marked routes, and easily identifiable campaign materials, such as flyers, brochures, and stickers. These materials should be visually appealing and concisely communicate your key message. Avoid overwhelming voters with excessive information; focus on one or two key talking points that resonate with their concerns. Consider incorporating visual aids, such as photos or infographics, to enhance the impact of your message. Moreover, providing your volunteers with tablets or smartphones pre-loaded with your voter database can significantly improve efficiency and data collection. This allows for real-time updates on voter contact and immediate feedback on the effectiveness of your canvassing efforts.

The actual canvassing process requires a systematic approach. Divide your target area into manageable sections, assigning each section to a team of volunteers. This ensures thorough coverage and avoids duplication of effort. Establish clear communication channels between your field teams and campaign headquarters, enabling real-time updates and problem-solving. Regular check-ins can help address challenges and ensure that volunteers stay motivated and engaged. And don't underestimate the power of team spirit. Encourage collaboration and celebrate successes to boost morale and maintain momentum throughout the campaign.

Data collection during canvassing is critical. Volunteers should meticulously document their interactions, including the voter's response to your message, any concerns raised, and any follow-up actions needed. This data is invaluable for refining your campaign strategy and identifying areas where you need to adjust your approach. Consider using a mobile app or a simplified data collection form to make this process as efficient as possible. This data allows for ongoing assessment and modification of your strategy.

Following up on canvassing efforts is equally important. After a canvassing event, you should immediately analyze the data collected to identify trends and areas needing improvement. For voters who expressed interest, a timely follow-up call or email can solidify their support. For those who expressed concerns, a personalized response addressing their specific issues demonstrates responsiveness and builds trust. This consistent communication keeps voters engaged and reinforces your campaign message.

Finally, don't overlook the importance of post-canvassing analysis. Reviewing the data collected allows you to assess the effectiveness of your strategy. Which messaging resonated most with voters? Where were your volunteers most successful? What challenges did they encounter? Use this information to optimize your future
canvassing efforts, ensuring a maximum impact on voter
engagement. By integrating feedback from volunteers and
continually refining your approach based on data analysis, you create a dynamic and responsive canvassing strategy that maximizes your chances of success.

Consider incorporating different canvassing techniques. For instance, you might organize themed canvasses, such as an environmental canvass focused on climate change or an economic canvass focusing on job creation and economic opportunities in your region. This targeted approach can resonate with specific voter segments more effectively. Additionally, consider partnering with local organizations or community groups to leverage their existing networks and reach new voters. This collaboration not only increases your reach but also demonstrates community engagement. Remember to always respect voter privacy and adhere to all relevant regulations during your canvassing operations.

Furthermore, you might experiment with different times of day for canvassing to optimize your contact rate. Some voters might be more accessible in the evenings, while others might be more receptive during the weekends. Adapting your canvassing schedule to the specific demographic you're targeting can greatly improve your efficiency. For example, canvassing during lunch hours in a business district might prove more productive than canvassing during the same time in a residential area. Testing different approaches and analyzing the results is essential to optimize the effectiveness of your efforts. The key is to be flexible and adaptable, constantly refining your approach based on the feedback you receive and the data you collect.

Another crucial aspect of effective canvassing is the effective deployment of your volunteers. You should assign volunteers to areas where their skills and experience are most valuable. For instance, those with strong communication skills can be assigned to more challenging interactions, while those with more experience can mentor newer volunteers. This careful allocation of resources ensures that your team is functioning at its optimal level. Don't forget to rotate assignments regularly to prevent burnout and maintain team motivation. By keeping your team engaged and energized, you ensure a higher quality of interaction with voters and a more effective canvassing operation. Regularly schedule team meetings to debrief on canvassing activities, share best practices, and address any challenges encountered in the field.

Finally, remember that effective canvassing is a continuous process of learning and adaptation. Regularly assess your progress, analyze the data you've collected, and make adjustments to your strategy as needed. This iterative approach ensures that you're always maximizing your impact and optimizing your resources. The goal isn't just to knock on doors; it's to build relationships, inspire voters, and ultimately, win the election. By combining a strategic approach with effective training, meticulous data collection, and a commitment to continuous improvement, you can transform your canvassing efforts into a powerful tool for electoral success. The detailed information gathered during canvassing is not just for the current election cycle; it's a valuable asset for future campaigns, providing insights into voter preferences and demographics. This ongoing data collection creates a robust and adaptable campaign structure.

Phone Banking and Voter Outreach

Building upon the groundwork laid by
effective canvassing, phone banking offers
another crucial avenue for direct voter
engagement. While face-to-face interactions
possess an undeniable personal touch, phone
banking allows for a broader reach, enabling
contact with a significantly larger segment
of the electorate in a shorter timeframe.
This scalability is a significant
advantage, particularly in
geographically dispersed districts or
when faced with time constraints.
However, the success of phone
banking hinges on meticulous
planning and execution.

The first step involves compiling a
comprehensive and accurate voter database.
This database should include contact
information, voter history (past voting
patterns, party affiliation, if available), and
any other relevant demographic data. The
quality of your database
directly impacts the effectiveness of your
phone banking efforts.

Inaccurate or incomplete information leads to wasted time and resources. Consider purchasing voter lists from reputable vendors, ensuring compliance with all relevant data privacy regulations. Supplement these purchased lists with information gathered during canvassing, ensuring a robust and up-to-date database.

Once the database is ready, recruit and train a team of skilled phone bankers. Effective phone banking requires more than just reading a script; it necessitates building rapport, actively listening to voter concerns, and adapting the conversation to individual needs. Train your team to handle objections gracefully, to effectively communicate the campaign's key messages, and to accurately record voter interactions. Role-playing exercises can significantly enhance their performance. Emphasize the importance of maintaining a positive and respectful tone, even when faced with criticism or resistance. Remember, every interaction, regardless of outcome, presents an opportunity to build goodwill and enhance the campaign's image. Regular feedback and coaching sessions ensure that your phone banking team remains highly effective and motivated.

The script itself plays a crucial role in the success of your phone banking efforts. It should be concise, compelling, and easy to follow. Avoid overly long or complex sentences. The script should highlight the candidate's key policy positions and personal story, emphasizing aspects most resonant with your target demographic. A multi-pronged approach, using slightly different scripts tailored to specific voter segments (e.g., young voters, senior citizens, etc.) can significantly increase effectiveness. Regularly evaluate the performance of your scripts and make adjustments based on feedback from your team. This ensures that your message resonates strongly with the intended audience.

Beyond the script, proper organization and tracking are vital for maximizing efficiency. Utilize a call tracking system to monitor call volume, talk time, and conversion rates. This data provides invaluable insights into the effectiveness of your phone banking efforts. Identify top performers and analyze their techniques to further refine your strategies. Track the responses to specific questions and concerns raised by voters, adjusting your approach to address recurring issues or objections. A well-organized system allows for real-time analysis and adjustments, maximizing your campaign's reach and impact.

Furthermore, integrating phone banking with other campaign
activities is crucial. Connect the information gathered through phone banking with data collected from canvassing and online interactions. This integrated approach creates a comprehensive profile of your target voters, allowing for highly targeted messaging and outreach. For example, voters who express interest in a particular policy issue during a phone bank call can be subsequently targeted with specific campaign literature or social media content. This synergistic
approach ensures that your efforts are not duplicated, but rather reinforce one
another.

The ethical considerations of phone banking should never be
overlooked. Strictly adhere to all applicable laws and regulations concerning telemarketing and voter contact. Respect voters' wishes; provide a clear and easy way for them to opt out of further

communication. Transparency is
paramount. Always clearly identify

yourself and your organization at the beginning of each call. Treat every interaction with respect and courtesy. Maintaining ethical standards not only complies with regulations, but also builds trust and strengthens the campaign's reputation.

Beyond simply making calls, use phone banking as an opportunity to recruit volunteers. During phone calls, gauge interest in volunteering, offering opportunities that align with the voter's expressed interests and availability. This transforms phone banking from a mere outreach tool into a potent volunteer recruitment strategy, amplifying the overall campaign effort.

Post-call analysis is just as important as the calls themselves.
Carefully review the notes and data collected by your phone banking team. Identify trends and patterns in voter responses. Analyze the effectiveness of different scripts and messaging strategies. Use this data to inform future phone banking efforts, fine-tuning your

approach for improved efficiency and increased voter engagement.
This continuous improvement cycle is crucial for maximizing the return on investment of your phone banking program.

Integrating technology is key for optimizing your phone banking program. Consider using automated dialer systems, which can significantly speed up the process and reduce manual labor.
However, ensure these systems comply with all relevant regulations to avoid penalties. Furthermore, explore using CRM (Customer Relationship Management) software to manage your voter database and track interactions. This technology allows for more efficient organization, more targeted messaging, and ultimately, a stronger connection with the voters.

Finally, remember that phone banking is not a standalone strategy.
It's most effective when used in conjunction with other voter
outreach methods, such as canvassing, email marketing, and social media engagement. A comprehensive, multi-faceted approach allows you to reach voters through their preferred channels, maximizing the impact of your campaign. Consistent and strategic

use of phone banking, integrated with other outreach activities, significantly increases voter engagement, strengthens the campaign's connection

with the community, and ultimately contributes to
electoral success.
By viewing phone banking as a crucial
component of a broader, multi-platform
voter engagement strategy, you can leverage
its power to connect with voters on a
personal level, build strong relationships,
and propel your campaign towards victory.

Organizing MeetandGreets and Community Events

Building on the personal connections forged through phone banking and canvassing, meet-and-greets and community events represent the next crucial step in grassroots organizing. These events are not merely opportunities to shake hands and pose for photos; they are carefully orchestrated strategies to build rapport, gather support, and demonstrate your commitment to the community. The effectiveness of these gatherings hinges on meticulous planning, thoughtful
execution, and a deep understanding of your target audience.

First, identify the ideal locations and times for your events. Consider the demographics of your target voters. A meet-and-greet at a bustling farmer's market will reach a different demographic than one held at a local senior center. Analyze voter registration data to
pinpoint areas with high concentrations of potential supporters. Timing is also crucial.

Weekday evenings might be ideal for
working professionals, while weekend
afternoons might attract families.
Avoid scheduling events during
major holidays or conflicting
community events.

Once you've chosen the location and time,
meticulously plan the logistics. Secure
necessary permits, if required. Arrange for
sufficient seating, refreshments (consider
dietary restrictions), and potentially a sound
system for speeches or presentations. Having
a clear agenda is essential, including planned
speaking points, opportunities for Q&A, and
designated areas for informal conversations.
Ensure adequate staffing – volunteers are
invaluable for guiding attendees, answering
questions, and managing logistics. Assign
specific roles and
responsibilities to each volunteer to avoid
confusion and ensure smooth operation.

The atmosphere you create is paramount.
Strive for a relaxed, welcoming
environment. Encourage genuine
interaction, allowing ample time for
personal conversations. Avoid overly
formal speeches; instead, opt for
conversational, relatable addresses that
highlight your core campaign messages.
Consider incorporating activities that

appeal to different age groups and interests. A

children's activity area at a family-friendly event, for example, can ease parental concerns and create a positive experience for everyone.

Choosing the right community events to participate in or sponsor is equally critical. Identify events that align with your campaign's values and resonate with your target audience. Sponsoring a local charity event, participating in a town hall meeting, or attending a community festival allows you to demonstrate your commitment to the community and interact with potential supporters in a relaxed setting. Your presence at these events should be genuine and
authentic; avoid appearing as though you are merely "checking a box." Engage genuinely with attendees, listen to their concerns, and demonstrate your understanding of their needs.

Don't underestimate the power of visual communication at these events. Have professionally designed banners, flyers, and other marketing materials readily available. These materials should clearly convey your campaign message, contact information, and website address. Consider incorporating photos and testimonials from local supporters to build trust and credibility. Ensure that all materials are consistent with your overall brand identity, maintaining a unified and professional image.

Following up after a meet-and-greet or community event is crucial for maximizing its impact. Within 24 to 48 hours, send a thank-you email to all attendees, reiterating your campaign message and including a link to your website or online donation platform. This follow-up reinforces the positive impression you made at the event and keeps your campaign top-of-mind. You can also use the data collected at the event to personalize future communication, tailoring your messages to the specific interests and concerns of different voter segments.

Moreover, analyze the event's performance post-event. Gather feedback from attendees and volunteers. What worked well? What could be improved? This feedback loop is vital for refining your strategy and maximizing the effectiveness of future events. Track metrics such as attendance, number of sign-ups, and donations received to measure the event's overall impact.

Let's delve into some practical examples. Imagine a candidate running for a local school board position. Organizing a meet-and-greet at a local school playground on a Saturday morning allows for interaction with parents and children. Having a face-painting station, a bouncy castle, and offering refreshments creates a welcoming atmosphere. The candidate can address parents' concerns regarding school safety, curriculum, and budget allocation in a conversational manner. Following the event, a thank-you email with links to the candidate's website and social media pages can reinforce the
connection.

Another example: A mayoral candidate organizing a town hall
meeting to discuss city-wide infrastructure improvements. This event provides a platform for the candidate to present their vision and engage directly with citizens. The town hall allows for a Q&A
session, enabling constituents to directly address their concerns regarding issues such as road repairs, public transportation, and waste management. Volunteers can

distribute campaign literature and collect contact information for future follow-up. Post-event, a
comprehensive summary of the meeting, including answers to
frequently asked questions, can be shared through email and on the candidate's website.

In another scenario, a congressional candidate might sponsor a local community cleanup event in a park. This demonstrates commitment to environmental conservation and provides opportunities for interaction with diverse segments of the community. The candidate can work alongside volunteers, demonstrating their dedication to public service. Following the cleanup, the candidate can send a thank-you email, highlighting the community's participation and their commitment to environmental stewardship.

For events targeting specific demographics, tailoring the approach is essential. A meet-and-greet targeted at senior citizens, for example, might be held at a senior center during the day, offering refreshments and comfortable seating. The candidate can discuss issues of
particular relevance to seniors, such as healthcare, social security, and retirement

planning. Utilizing volunteers from the senior

community itself can build trust and create a warm, welcoming atmosphere. Similarly, a candidate seeking to engage young voters might organize an event at a local college campus, featuring a panel discussion with students, or a town hall with relevant speakers. Offering free food and entertainment can be effective incentives to attract a larger audience.

Finally, remember that the success of meet-and-greets and
community events isn't solely measured by attendance figures. It's about building relationships, fostering trust, and demonstrating your genuine commitment to the community. By creating welcoming and engaging environments, listening to the concerns of your
constituents, and consistently following up, you can transform these events from simple gatherings into powerful tools for voter engagement and campaign success. Strategic planning, thoughtful execution, and consistent follow-up are the cornerstones of converting meet-and-greets and community events from mere
opportunities into genuine pathways to victory. These interactions cultivate a sense

of personal connection, crucial for building a
robust foundation of support in the final
push to election day.

Getting Out the Vote GOTV Strategies

Building upon the groundwork laid through personal interactions and community engagement, the final and arguably most critical phase of any successful campaign is Getting Out the Vote (GOTV). This isn't simply about encouraging people to vote; it's about a meticulously planned and executed operation to ensure your supporters actually make it to the polls. GOTV strategies are the culmination of all previous efforts, a symphony of coordinated actions designed to maximize turnout on Election Day.

The success of your GOTV operation hinges on accurate data. Before you even begin thinking about mobilization, you need a robust voter database. This database should contain not just names and addresses, but also crucial information about voter history, party affiliation (if available and relevant to your jurisdiction), likely voting preferences based on past elections and any publicly available information, and contact information including phone numbers and email addresses.

Regularly updating this database is critical; people move, change phone numbers, and their political affiliations can shift over time. Investing in voter file software that allows for regular updates and targeted segmentation is an essential campaign expense.

Identifying your most likely voters is crucial. This isn't about targeting only your most ardent supporters; it's about focusing your resources on those most likely to vote and those most persuadable. Use your voter database to segment your electorate. Identify your "likely voters"—those who have consistently voted in previous elections. These individuals require less intensive GOTV efforts, but they still need a reminder to vote and confirmation of polling place information. Then identify your "persuadable voters" – those who lean towards your candidate but may not always vote. These individuals require a different, more personalized approach. Finally, you will have those who are unlikely to vote for you; while they aren't a focus of your GOTV operation, you may want to identify those who are highly likely to vote for your opponent, perhaps for targeted counter-messaging.

With your database segmented, you can begin implementing various GOTV strategies. These strategies should be multi-faceted and tailored to the specific needs of each voter segment.

Phone banking remains a powerful GOTV tool, particularly effective for reaching older voters or those less engaged with technology.
However, simply calling and asking people to vote is insufficient.
Trained volunteers should engage in personalized conversations, reminding voters of your candidate's platform and highlighting the importance of their participation. These calls should be short, focused and personalized based on the information you have
collected about each voter. For example, a call to a voter who is concerned about local schools could highlight your candidate's commitment to education funding.
Sophisticated phone banking systems allow for automated call scheduling, tracking and reporting –making this process significantly more efficient. Furthermore, A/B testing different scripts and call approaches can allow you to fine-tune the messaging for

optimal results. Finally, a robust call tracking system allows you to manage your volunteers' workload effectively and get real-time feedback on campaign progress.

Text messaging, another powerful tool, allows for rapid communication with a large number of voters. Short, impactful texts reminding voters about election day, providing polling location information, and including a link to a candidate's website can be highly effective. Again, personalization is key; segmenting your text message lists and crafting unique messages for each group can dramatically improve response rates. Furthermore, sophisticated text messaging platforms allow for two-way communication, allowing your campaign to address voters' questions and concerns in real-time.
The key is to use text messages sparingly, avoiding excessive communication which could annoy voters and lead to opt-outs.

Email remains a valuable tool, particularly for disseminating detailed information about your candidate and their platform. Emails can contain longer messages, links to campaign videos, and details about polling locations and voter registration deadlines. However, unlike texts, emails can easily be ignored, so clear, concise language and a compelling subject line are crucial. Email marketing tools allow you

to track open rates, click-through
rates, and other key metrics, helping
you to refine your email strategy
over time.

In-person canvassing, despite the rise of
digital communication, retains its
importance in GOTV. A personal visit from
a volunteer can be a powerful reminder to
vote and an opportunity to address any last-
minute concerns. Canvassers should be well-
trained and
equipped with clear instructions and
materials. They should know the best times
to visit voters, what message points to
emphasize, and how to handle objections.
GPS-enabled devices can help optimize
canvassing routes, and dedicated canvassing
apps allow for real-time data collection and
tracking of voter interactions. The key to
successful canvassing is to make it efficient
and effective; focusing your efforts on the
most persuadable voters and tracking your
progress in real-time.

Beyond these core strategies, several
additional tactics can enhance your
GOTV efforts. For example, offering
rides to the polls can be particularly

effective for voters who lack transportation. Partnering with local community groups and organizations can help you reach voters who may be harder to contact through other means. Organizing "Election Day rallies" or "vote parties" near polling places can build enthusiasm and encourage voters to participate. Consider social media strategies, targeting ads based on the segments of your audience who are still uncontacted.

Monitoring and adapting are crucial throughout the GOTV process. Track your progress in real-time, analyzing response rates, identifying any issues, and making adjustments as needed. Regular team meetings are vital to review data, share successes, and address challenges. It's important to have a clear chain of command and a system for escalating issues to resolve problems efficiently. The goal is to have a flexible operation that can quickly respond to changing conditions.

Finally, don't underestimate the power of simple, personalized communication. A handwritten postcard or a phone call from a trusted friend or community leader can be surprisingly effective in encouraging voters to participate. Personalization can significantly boost engagement and motivate voters to turn out on election day.

Effective GOTV requires detailed planning, meticulous execution, and a constant focus on reaching out to voters and encouraging them to exercise their right to vote. It's the culmination of months, even years, of groundwork, translating all previous efforts into tangible results. Through a multi-faceted approach that leverages technology, personal connections and community engagement, a robust GOTV operation can significantly increase voter turnout and ultimately determine the success or failure of a campaign. Remember that a strong GOTV strategy isn't simply about numbers; it's about
engaging the community, motivating voters, and ensuring every voice is heard.

Creating Professional Campaign Literature Using Canva

Canva offers a user-friendly interface, making it accessible even for those with limited design experience. Its drag-and-drop functionality allows for easy manipulation of elements, and its extensive library of templates, images, and fonts provides a wealth of options to create professional-looking materials without requiring advanced design skills. This is particularly valuable for political campaigns operating on tight budgets, where hiring a professional graphic designer might be financially unfeasible.

Before diving into Canva, it's crucial to define the purpose of your campaign literature. What message are you trying to convey? Who is your target audience? Understanding these questions will guide your design choices. For example, a flyer aimed at younger voters might employ a more modern and vibrant aesthetic, while a brochure

targeting older voters might opt for a cleaner, more traditional design.
Consider the overall tone of your campaign: is it serious and authoritative, or more playful and approachable? This tonal consistency needs to reflect across all your campaign materials.

Once you have a clear understanding of your goals and target
audience, you can begin designing in Canva. Start by selecting a template that aligns with your campaign's aesthetic and message. Canva offers a vast collection of pre-designed templates, categorized by various themes and purposes. These templates provide a solid foundation, saving you time and effort in the initial design phase.
However, don't be afraid to customize them to reflect your
campaign's unique identity. Remember, the goal is to create materials that are not only visually appealing but also clearly communicate your message.

Next, consider the content of your campaign materials. Keep it concise and impactful.
Use strong verbs and avoid jargon. Focus on the key messages you want voters to remember. Use bullet points and short paragraphs to make the information easily

digestible. Include a clear call to action, whether it's to visit your website, volunteer for your campaign, or donate to your cause. Strong visuals are crucial;

utilize high-quality images and graphics that resonate with your target audience. Canva provides access to a vast library of stock photos, but you can also upload your own images. Ensure that all images are high-resolution and professionally presented to avoid a low-quality appearance.

When choosing fonts, opt for readability over stylistic flourishes. Select fonts that are easy to read, even at smaller sizes. Avoid using too many different fonts, as this can make your design look cluttered and unprofessional. Stick to two or three fonts at most, choosing one for headings and another for body text. Canva provides a wide selection of fonts, allowing you to choose those that best represent your campaign's brand. Experiment with different font pairings to find a combination that works well together.

Color is another important aspect of design. Use colors that are consistent with your campaign's branding. Consider the psychological impact of different colors; for example, blue often conveys trust and stability, while red can evoke energy and passion. However, avoid using too many colors, as this can make your design appear overwhelming. Stick to a limited palette of two or three colors, using them consistently throughout your materials.

Once you have finalized your design, it's crucial to thoroughly review it before publication or printing. Check for spelling and grammar errors, ensuring that all information is accurate and up-to-date. Review the layout and ensure that all elements are balanced and visually appealing. Seek feedback from trusted colleagues or
campaign team members to get an outside perspective on your
design. Their fresh eyes can often catch mistakes or areas for
improvement that you might have overlooked.

For printing, Canva provides options to download your designs in various formats, including high-resolution PDFs suitable for professional printing. When selecting a printing service, ensure they offer high-quality printing and finishing options to enhance the overall impact of your campaign literature. Before committing to a large print run, it's wise to print a few test copies to ensure you are satisfied with the final product's color accuracy and quality.

Beyond brochures and flyers, Canva can be instrumental in designing other campaign materials. Consider creating visually appealing social media graphics to accompany your online posts. Canva provides templates specifically optimized for different social media platforms, ensuring your graphics are appropriately sized and formatted. Design eye-catching yard signs and posters that will grab attention and effectively promote your campaign. These visible representations of your campaign can significantly contribute to local outreach and brand recognition.

Canva's versatility extends to creating compelling email headers and templates. Consistent branding across all communication channels reinforces your campaign's identity and messaging. A well-designed email header can significantly improve open rates and engagement. Use Canva to create professional-looking headers that incorporate your campaign's logo, colors, and overall aesthetic.

Remember that consistency in design is crucial across all campaign materials. Use the same logo, fonts, and color palette across all your brochures, flyers, social media graphics, and email headers. This creates a cohesive brand identity and reinforces your campaign's message. Your campaign's visual identity should be easily recognizable and memorable, allowing voters to quickly associate your materials with your candidate and platform.

Don't underestimate the power of simple, well-designed campaign materials. They are an invaluable tool for disseminating your message, engaging voters, and ultimately, winning the election. By utilizing Canva's resources and following the design principles outlined above, you can create professional-looking materials that will effectively communicate your campaign's message and leave a lasting impression on voters. Regularly analyze the effectiveness of your materials; track which designs generate the most engagement and adapt your future designs based on data-driven insights. Continuously refining your design strategies is crucial for optimal campaign success. Moreover, consider A/B testing different designs to see which resonates most effectively with your target demographic. This data-driven approach will ensure your materials

are as effective as possible. Ultimately, the
goal is to create campaign literature that is
not only aesthetically pleasing but also
highly
effective in communicating your campaign's
message and achieving its objectives.

Writing Compelling Campaign Slogans and Taglines

Crafting a compelling campaign slogan or tagline is far more than just coming up with a catchy phrase. It's about distilling the essence of your campaign, your candidate's vision, and your core message into a few memorable words that will stick with voters long after they've seen your flyer or heard your advertisement. This short, impactful statement acts as a cornerstone of your campaign's branding, guiding all other communication efforts and reinforcing your key message across various media.

The process begins with a deep understanding of your candidate and their platform. What are their key policy positions? What are their core values? What unique qualities or experiences set them apart from their opponents? These questions must be thoroughly addressed before even considering potential slogans. A slogan born out of a genuine understanding of the candidate's strengths and the electorate's concerns will resonate far more authentically than a generic, manufactured phrase.

Consider the tone and style you want to project. Do you aim for a serious and authoritative voice, or a more approachable and relatable one? A youthful candidate might benefit from a more energetic and modern tagline, while a seasoned politician might opt for a more traditional and dignified approach. The overall tone should be
consistent with the candidate's personality and the overall campaign aesthetic. Analyzing your target demographic is crucial in this decision-making process. Different slogans will resonate with different age groups and socio-economic backgrounds.
Understanding your audience is paramount in selecting a slogan that truly connects.

Brainstorming sessions are invaluable at this stage. Gather your campaign team, including volunteers and key advisors, and generate as many ideas as possible, regardless of how outlandish they may initially seem. Encourage creativity and avoid self-censorship. The goal is to generate a wide pool of options to choose from later. This collaborative approach will foster a sense of ownership and

commitment to the final chosen slogan. Use mind mapping
techniques or even free-writing exercises to unlock fresh perspectives and unexpected ideas.

Once you have a substantial list of potential slogans, it's time to refine and evaluate. Consider these crucial factors:

Memorability:
Is the slogan easy to remember and recall? A simple, concise phrase is far more likely to resonate with voters than a long and complicated one. Consider using alliteration, rhyme, or other poetic devices to enhance memorability. A memorable slogan has the power to become a rallying cry, a shorthand for your campaign's message.

Clarity:
Does the slogan clearly convey the candidate's message and key policy positions? Avoid ambiguous language or jargon that could confuse voters. The meaning should be readily apparent, without needing extensive explanation. Clarity ensures the message is

delivered effectively and understood by the target audience.

Uniqueness:
Does the slogan stand out from those used by other campaigns? A unique and original slogan will help your campaign stand out from the crowd and create a distinctive brand identity. Research what your opponents are using to avoid any unintended similarities or unintentional conflicts.

Relevance:
Does the slogan resonate with the concerns and priorities of your target voters? A slogan must address the needs and desires of the electorate. It needs to tap into prevailing sentiments and offer solutions to the challenges faced by the community.

Testability:
Before settling on a final slogan, test it on focus groups to gauge their reaction. Gather feedback on its effectiveness, memorability, and overall impact. This empirical feedback is essential in making informed decisions. Consider A/B testing various slogans to directly compare their relative effectiveness.

Once you have selected your top contenders, conduct rigorous testing.

Use online surveys, focus groups, and informal polls to

gather feedback on how each slogan resonates with different
segments of your target audience. Pay close attention to the
emotional responses the slogans evoke. A slogan that evokes positive feelings is far more likely to be successful than one that elicits
negative or indifferent reactions. This data-driven approach is vital for optimizing your selection and ensuring maximum campaign impact.

Consider also the visual aspects. How does the slogan look in various formats? Will it work effectively on a campaign button, a banner, a social media post, or a television advertisement? The visual appeal of the slogan should be just as carefully considered as its verbal impact.

After careful consideration and thorough testing, select your
campaign slogan. Once chosen, it should be consistently used across all campaign materials, from website banners to email signatures to billboards. Consistency is key to reinforcing the message and
building brand recognition. The chosen

slogan should guide the overall tone and messaging of the campaign, ensuring all communication efforts remain on-message and cohesive.

Remember, a successful campaign slogan is more than just a catchy phrase; it's a powerful tool that can shape public perception, inspire voters, and ultimately contribute to a successful election outcome. Investing the necessary time and resources in crafting a compelling slogan is an investment in the overall success of your campaign. The impact of a well-crafted slogan can be far-reaching and long-lasting, contributing significantly to the overall success of your campaign. A truly resonant slogan can become synonymous with the candidate themselves, shaping the public perception of the candidate and driving voter engagement.

Designing Effective Yard Signs and Posters

Building on the foundation of a strong campaign slogan, the next crucial step in effective communication is the design and deployment of compelling yard signs and posters. These seemingly simple tools are powerful visual aids that can significantly impact voter

perception and turnout. A well-designed sign isn't just a piece of cardboard; it's a miniature billboard, a constant reminder of your candidate and their message, working tirelessly even while you sleep.
Ignoring this aspect of your campaign is a missed opportunity to engage potential voters in a highly visible and cost-effective manner.

The first consideration is the
size and placement
of your signs. Overly large signs can appear intrusive or even illegal depending on local ordinances. Check with your local election board to understand size restrictions and permitted placement areas. Generally, standard yard sign sizes are

effective and readily available from print shops.

Too small, however, and your message might be lost in the visual clutter of a neighborhood. Strategic placement is key – high-traffic areas, near intersections, and in visible locations along main roads are ideal. However, always obtain permission from property owners before placing signs on private property to avoid any legal issues and maintain positive community relations. Remember, respecting

property rights shows respect for the community you are trying to win over.

Next comes the
design itself
. Simplicity reigns supreme. Avoid overcrowding the sign with too much text or graphics. A clear, concise message is far more effective than a cluttered design. Think of your sign as an advertisement; it needs to grab attention quickly. Your campaign slogan, ideally, should take center stage, followed by the candidate's name and perhaps a key policy position or two. Use a strong, easily readable font, preferably sans-serif, and choose colors that are both eye-catching and reflect the campaign's overall

branding. A consistent color scheme across all campaign materials (signs, posters, brochures, etc.) creates a unified and memorable brand identity.

High-quality printing
is also non-negotiable. A faded, low-
resolution sign looks unprofessional and
can damage your
campaign's credibility. Invest in durable
materials that can withstand the elements,
especially if the campaign runs for an
extended period. Consider using weather-
resistant inks and materials to ensure your
message remains clear and legible
throughout the campaign. Think about the
longevity of your investment; a durable
sign that lasts the entire campaign is far
more cost-effective than replacing multiple
faded or damaged ones.

For posters, the principles remain similar,
but the design possibilities expand slightly.
Posters, often larger than yard signs, can
accommodate a more detailed message or
imagery. However, the key to effective
poster design is still clarity and conciseness.
Consider using compelling visuals –
photographs of the candidate interacting
with voters, graphic representations of key
policy proposals, or symbolic imagery
related to your campaign's platform. These
visuals can enhance the impact of your
written message and create a more engaging

experience for potential voters. The same principles of font choice, color scheme consistency, and high-quality printing apply equally to posters as they do to yard signs.

Target your audience:
The design should speak to the specific demographics you're trying to reach. A campaign targeting younger voters might employ a more modern, visually dynamic design compared to a campaign appealing to a more mature electorate.
Research your target audience's preferences and tailor the design accordingly. This could involve using different color schemes, fonts, or imagery to resonate with specific groups. Testing different designs in focus groups can provide invaluable insight into what resonates best with potential voters before you commit to large-scale printing.

Beyond the design elements, the **strategic deployment** of your signs and posters matters just as much. Conduct thorough research to determine the most effective locations for your materials.
Concentrate your efforts in areas with high voter turnout and significant concentrations of your target demographic. Collaborate with your campaign volunteers to identify strategic

placement locations and ensure proper
and legal distribution of campaign

materials. Regularly check your signs and posters for damage or vandalism and replace or repair them promptly to maintain a consistent and professional image.

Furthermore, consider **integrating your signs and posters with other campaign initiatives.** For instance, you can include your website URL, social media handles, or QR codes that link to your campaign website. This allows your signs and posters to seamlessly integrate with your digital campaign strategy, driving traffic to your online platforms and expanding the reach of your message. This synergistic approach maximizes the effectiveness of both your physical and digital communication strategies.

Finally, don't underestimate the impact of **consistent branding.** Your signs and posters should reflect the overall look and feel of your entire campaign. This means maintaining consistent color palettes, fonts, and imagery across all your materials, from your website to your brochures to your social media posts.

Consistent branding creates a cohesive and memorable identity for your campaign, reinforcing your message and making it easier for voters to associate it with your candidate. This unified image establishes a strong brand recognition, enhancing the recall and positive association with your campaign. Think of Nike's swoosh or Apple's apple – simple,
memorable, and instantly recognizable. Strive for the same impact with your campaign's visual identity.

In conclusion, designing effective yard signs and posters is not a trivial task; it is a critical component of a successful campaign. Investing time, resources, and careful consideration into the design, placement, and overall strategy of these simple materials can significantly impact the outcome of your election. By following these best practices, you can transform these seemingly minor campaign tools into powerful instruments that amplify your message and connect with voters in a tangible and impactful way. Remember, a well-designed sign isn't just a piece of printed material; it's a silent but powerful ambassador for your candidate, working tirelessly to build support and win votes. It's a visual representation of your campaign's core message, speaking volumes even without a single word uttered. Pay

close attention to every detail, from the font
choice

to the placement strategy, and you will reap
significant rewards come election day.

Creating Engaging Social Media Graphics

Building upon the effectiveness of physical campaign materials like yard signs and posters, we now turn our attention to the digital realm: social media. In today's interconnected world, a strong online presence is no longer a luxury, but a necessity for any successful political campaign. While traditional methods remain important, social media provides a direct line of communication to a vast and diverse electorate, allowing for immediate feedback and targeted messaging. However, simply having a social media presence isn't enough; you need to capture attention in a crowded digital landscape, and that starts with creating engaging social media graphics.

The key to effective social media graphics lies in understanding your target audience and tailoring your visuals to resonate with their values and interests. A graphic designed to appeal to younger voters, for instance, will differ significantly from one aimed at older

demographics. Consider the platforms you are using as well.
Instagram, with its emphasis on visual storytelling, requires a different approach than Twitter, where brevity and impact are paramount.

Before diving into design specifics, it's crucial to define your brand identity. This includes your campaign's colors, fonts, and overall aesthetic. Consistency is key; your graphics should look and feel cohesive, reinforcing your campaign's message and creating a
recognizable brand. This consistent branding helps establish trust and familiarity with your audience, making your campaign more memorable and trustworthy. Use your campaign's logo consistently across all platforms and maintain a unified color palette to solidify brand recognition. A strong brand identity acts as a silent spokesperson, conveying professionalism and competence even before a single word is read.

Once your brand identity is established, you can begin creating compelling graphics. High-quality images and videos are essential. Poorly lit, blurry, or unprofessional-looking images can

undermine your credibility. Invest in
professional photography or use high-

resolution stock photos that align with your campaign's messaging.
Avoid generic or clichéd imagery. Instead, opt for images that are authentic, relatable, and evoke emotion. Think about using images that show the candidate interacting with constituents, participating in community events, or demonstrating their commitment to the issues. Authenticity builds trust.

The choice of fonts is equally important. Select fonts that are easy to read and reflect your campaign's personality. Avoid using too many different fonts in a single graphic, as this can appear cluttered and unprofessional. Stick to 1-2 fonts maximum, ensuring a clear hierarchy of importance in your text. Legibility is crucial, especially on smaller screens. A font that looks good on a desktop computer may be difficult to read on a smartphone.

When designing graphics, keep it simple and concise. Avoid overwhelming viewers with too much text or information. A cluttered graphic is less likely to be noticed

or remembered. Focus on conveying a
single, clear message. Use visual cues, such
as strong colors and compelling imagery, to
reinforce your message without relying
solely on text. Remember, less is often more
in graphic design.

Social media platforms have specific image size
requirements.
Failing to adhere to these guidelines can
result in your graphics appearing cropped
or distorted. Always check the platform's
specifications before uploading your
designs. This seemingly minor detail is
often overlooked, resulting in
unprofessional-looking posts that fail to
capture attention.

Consider using design tools like Canva,
Adobe Photoshop, or Illustrator. Canva, in
particular, offers a user-friendly interface
and a vast library of templates, making it
an accessible option even for those without
professional design experience. These tools
provide ready-made templates and
resources to create visually appealing
graphics quickly and efficiently. However,
even with user-friendly tools,
understanding basic design principles
remains crucial. Learn the basics of color
theory, typography, and composition to
create more effective visuals.

Beyond the technical aspects, consider the emotional impact of your graphics. Do your images and videos evoke the feelings you want to associate with your campaign? Positive emotions, such as hope, optimism, and community, are generally more effective than negative emotions like fear or anger. However, depending on your campaign's message, a well-placed image evoking concern or urgency might be effective, but it should be handled carefully and strategically.

Incorporating data and statistics into your graphics can also be a powerful strategy, particularly when focusing on specific policy proposals. However, present the data clearly and concisely, using charts and graphs to make it easily digestible. Avoid overwhelming viewers with complex data sets.

A/B testing is crucial for optimizing your social media graphics.
Create multiple versions of the same graphic, each with slight variations (different images, colors, or text), and track their

performance. Analyze which versions generate the most engagement and use the data to inform future designs. This iterative process ensures constant improvement and refinement of your visual communication.

Finally, don't forget the importance of social media advertising. Paid campaigns can significantly amplify the reach of your graphics, ensuring that your message is seen by a wider audience. While organic reach is important, paid advertising provides a valuable supplement. Target your advertising carefully, selecting demographics and interests that align with your target voters.

Creating engaging social media graphics is an iterative process requiring continuous refinement and optimization. It is not merely about creating aesthetically pleasing images; it's about crafting visual narratives that connect with your audience on an emotional level, effectively communicate your campaign's message, and ultimately drive voter engagement. By understanding your audience, adhering to design principles, and leveraging the power of data-driven decision-making, you can transform your social media presence into a powerful engine for political success. Remember, your social media graphics are not just visuals; they are the face of your campaign in the digital world. Make them count. The effort you invest in crafting compelling visuals will directly translate into increased awareness, greater voter engagement, and ultimately, a stronger campaign. Don't underestimate the power of a well-designed graphic to sway public opinion. It's a visual testament to your campaign's message, silently speaking volumes to your audience. The investment in time and resources will be repaid tenfold in the impact you achieve.

Consistent, high-quality visuals are an investment in the success of your campaign, making them as critical as any other aspect of your strategy.

Utilizing Video and Multimedia in your Campaign

Building on the foundation of a strong social media presence, the next crucial element in a modern political campaign is the strategic use of video and multimedia. While static images are important for grabbing attention, video offers a far more dynamic and engaging way to connect with voters. It allows you to convey personality, build trust, and articulate your message in a way that resonates deeply. In today's fast-paced media environment, short, impactful videos are more likely to capture attention spans than lengthy written pieces or even detailed infographics.

The first step is identifying the platforms best suited to your target demographic. While YouTube remains a powerful video-sharing platform with a broad reach, platforms like TikTok, Instagram Reels, and Facebook are often better for reaching younger voters.
Understanding the nuances of each platform is vital. TikTok, for example, favors short,

highly engaging clips often driven by trending sounds or challenges. This requires a different approach than a longer, more formal address on YouTube. Instagram Reels, similarly, benefits from visually appealing, fast-paced content. Facebook, while broader in its audience, still rewards engaging content that encourages comments, shares, and interaction. A multi-platform strategy, tailored to each platform's audience and conventions, is key.

The content itself must be carefully planned. Consider a mix of approaches. Short, impactful "behind-the-scenes" clips offer a glimpse into your personality and daily life, humanizing your campaign and making you relatable to voters. These can be as simple as a short video of you interacting with supporters at a local event, visiting a small business, or working in your community. Authenticity is key here – avoid anything that feels staged or artificial. The goal is to show the real you, connecting with voters on a personal level.

Policy-focused videos can also be incredibly effective, but they need to be concise and engaging. Avoid dry, monotone presentations. Instead, use strong visuals, compelling narratives, and clear language to explain your positions. Consider using infographics or animated sequences to simplify complex topics, making them easily digestible for a wider audience. Interviews with constituents or experts who support your policy positions can add credibility and further engage your audience. A series of short videos addressing specific issues is often more effective than one long, rambling video covering a range of topics. The goal is to break down complex information into easily digestible chunks.

Live streams offer an opportunity for real-time engagement with voters. These can be used for question-and-answer sessions, announcements, or even casual conversations. The interactive nature of live streams fosters a sense of community and allows you to directly address voter concerns. Careful preparation is crucial here; having a clear plan, engaging visuals, and a moderator to field questions smoothly can make the difference between a successful live stream and a chaotic disaster. Remember to monitor the comments section and address relevant questions throughout the stream.

Responding in real time shows your willingness to engage, enhancing voter perception of your campaign.

Beyond individual videos, consider developing a series of thematic videos. This could include a series focusing on your key policy positions, or a series highlighting your interactions with constituents across different communities. This type of structured approach allows you to build a cohesive narrative, reinforce your key
messages, and keep your audience engaged. A strategic series helps create a consistent brand and a regular engagement cadence.

Multimedia content expands your reach beyond traditional video formats. Infographics, for example, can condense complex
information into a visually appealing format that is easily shared across social media. Podcasts, while requiring a different approach, offer an intimate and engaging way to connect with voters. Podcasts allow for deeper dives into policy positions, longer discussions, and a more relaxed conversational tone. Consider partnering with local media outlets to create podcast episodes that are relevant to the community.

The key is to integrate these different media channels,

linking them to each other and cross-promoting across various platforms.

Effective use of video and multimedia requires a strategic approach to promotion. Boosting your videos on social media platforms is a critical component of expanding their reach beyond your immediate followers. Targeted advertising allows you to focus your spending on the demographics most likely to respond positively to your message.
Tracking your video analytics is also essential to measuring effectiveness and refining your approach.
Understanding which videos resonate most with which demographics allows for future strategic refinement of content.

However, creating and distributing high-quality video and
multimedia content requires resources and technical expertise. This may involve hiring a professional videographer or editor, using sophisticated video editing software, or contracting with a digital marketing agency specializing in political campaigns. While these services can be

costly, the investment can pay huge dividends in terms of increased voter engagement, positive brand image, and ultimately, electoral success. Strategic outsourcing can be a valuable approach; allocating responsibilities based on your resources allows for maximizing results.

Finally, remember the importance of accessibility. Ensure your videos are captioned for viewers with hearing impairments, and consider creating versions in multiple languages to reach a diverse electorate. Accessibility is not simply a matter of compliance; it's about inclusivity and ensuring everyone has equal access to your message. It demonstrates your commitment to equity and broad representation, strengthening voter trust and promoting a strong, ethical brand identity.

In conclusion, integrating video and multimedia into your campaign is not merely a trend; it's a necessity in the modern political
landscape. By strategically leveraging different platforms, employing a diverse range of content formats, and focusing on consistent, high-quality production, you can significantly enhance your reach, strengthen voter engagement, and maximize your chances of

electoral success. Remember, the goal isn't simply to create videos; it's to use them to build relationships, communicate effectively, and ultimately, win the hearts and minds of the voters. The effort invested will undoubtedly contribute to the overall success of your campaign.
Careful planning, consistent execution, and adaptation to the
changing digital landscape are essential
for reaping the full rewards of this critical campaign tool.

Search Engine Optimization SEO for Campaigns

Search engine optimization (SEO) is paramount for a successful political campaign in today's digital landscape. Voters increasingly rely on online searches to find information about candidates, platforms, and upcoming elections. A strong SEO strategy ensures your campaign website and related content rank highly in search engine results pages (SERPs), maximizing visibility and reach. This translates directly to increased voter engagement and ultimately, a greater chance of electoral success.

The first step involves keyword research. This isn't simply about brainstorming words related to your campaign; it's about understanding what voters are
actually
searching for. Tools like Google Keyword Planner, Ahrefs, SEMrush, and even simple Google Autocomplete can reveal valuable insights. Consider keywords related to your name, your political party, your district or

state, relevant policy issues, and even your opponent's name. Don't limit yourself to obvious terms; explore long-tail keywords – longer, more specific phrases – that reflect nuanced voter queries. For example, instead of just "election results," you might target "election results [your state] 2024" or "local election results [your city]". The more specific your keywords, the more targeted your reach will be.

Once you've identified your target keywords, integrate them naturally into your website content. Avoid keyword stuffing, a tactic that involves cramming keywords into text without regard for readability.
Search engines penalize this practice, leading to lower rankings.
Instead, focus on creating high-quality, informative content that genuinely addresses voter concerns and uses keywords organically within a natural writing flow. This includes your website copy, blog posts, press releases, and any other online materials.

Your website itself must be optimized for search engines. This begins with a well-structured website that's easy to navigate. Ensure your website is mobile-friendly, as a significant portion of online searches are conducted on smartphones and tablets. Search engines prioritize mobile-friendly sites in their rankings. Use clear, concise headings

and subheadings (H1, H2, H3 tags) to structure your content
logically, making it easier for both users and search engines to understand. Compelling visuals, such as high-quality images and videos, not only enhance user experience but can also improve SEO. Ensure your images are optimized with descriptive alt text, which helps search engines understand the image content.

Link building is another crucial element of SEO. Earn high-quality backlinks from reputable websites relevant to your campaign or political sphere. Backlinks are essentially votes of confidence from other sites, signaling to search engines that your content is valuable and trustworthy. This isn't about buying backlinks; that's a black hat SEO tactic that can hurt your rankings. Instead, focus on building relationships with relevant organizations, media outlets, and
community groups that may link back to your website naturally. Guest blogging on relevant websites can be an effective way to earn backlinks, as long as it's done ethically and focuses on providing genuine value to the host site's audience.

Local SEO is especially important for local or state-level campaigns.
Ensure your campaign website's information is accurate and consistent across all online platforms, including Google My Business, which allows you to create a free business profile that appears in local search results. Include your address, phone number, and hours of operation on your website and all online listings.
Encourage voters to leave reviews on your Google My Business profile; positive reviews can significantly boost your local SEO. If you're focusing on a specific geographic area, incorporating location-based keywords into your website content can improve your visibility in local searches.

Technical SEO is often overlooked, but it's essential for a well-optimized website. Ensure your website is fast-loading, as slow-loading sites negatively impact user experience and SEO rankings. Optimize your website's code for efficiency and use a content delivery network (CDN) to improve load times. Make sure your website is properly structured and uses a sitemap (XML sitemap) to help search engines crawl and index your content. A regularly updated and well-maintained website demonstrates commitment and credibility, boosting trust and potentially enhancing rankings.

Regularly monitor your SEO performance. Use Google Analytics and Google Search Console to track your website's ranking, traffic, and other key metrics. This will help you identify what's working, what's not, and provide data-driven insights to refine your strategy over time. Don't be afraid to adapt your strategy based on your performance data. SEO is not a one-time task; it's an ongoing process that requires constant monitoring and adjustment to keep your campaign at the forefront of search results.

Beyond the website, SEO extends to other aspects of your digital presence. Ensure your social media profiles are optimized with relevant keywords in your bios and descriptions. Utilize relevant hashtags to increase the visibility of your social media posts. Create high-quality content on social media platforms that aligns with your website's SEO strategy. Consistency is key; regularly posting
valuable content helps reinforce your

online presence and signal relevance to search engines.

Consider the role of schema markup. Schema markup is a type of code that helps search engines understand the content of your website. It allows you to provide additional context and information about your candidate, campaign, and events. This can lead to rich snippets in search results, increasing click-through rates and ultimately, voter engagement. Implement schema markup
strategically across your website to enhance your search engine visibility and improve user experience.

Paid search advertising, such as Google Ads, can supplement your SEO efforts. While SEO focuses on organic rankings, paid advertising allows you to buy your way to the top of search results. This can be particularly useful in the weeks leading up to an election, when visibility is critical. Target your ads carefully, focusing on specific keywords and demographics to maximize your return on investment. Carefully track your paid search campaigns to ensure your budget is being spent effectively.

The effectiveness of your SEO strategy is directly tied to the quality and relevance of your content. Focus on creating high-quality, informative content that genuinely addresses voter concerns and interests. This will naturally incorporate keywords, improve your rankings, and boost engagement. Remember, the goal is not just to rank highly in search results, but to connect with voters and persuade them to support your campaign. A successful SEO strategy is just one component of a broader, comprehensive digital marketing plan, all working together towards a common goal: electoral victory.
By focusing on delivering valuable content, building strong
relationships, and continuously refining your strategies based on data, your campaign will be well-positioned to maximize its digital reach and achieve success. Remember to always adhere to ethical SEO practices; avoid black hat tactics that can harm your campaign's reputation and ultimately hurt your chances of winning.

Paid Social Media Advertising

Building upon a robust SEO strategy, paid social media advertising represents the next crucial layer in a comprehensive digital campaign. While organic social media engagement is vital for
building community and fostering direct interaction with voters, paid advertising allows for targeted outreach to specific demographic groups, significantly amplifying your message and increasing the likelihood of securing votes. The key to successful paid social media advertising lies in strategic planning, precise targeting, and meticulous monitoring of results.

First, define your target audience. Avoid broad strokes. Instead, leverage the detailed demographic data available through platforms like Facebook, Instagram, Twitter, and TikTok. Consider factors like age, location, interests, political affiliations, and even online
behaviors. For example, a candidate running on a platform of
environmental protection might target users

who follow
environmental organizations, frequently
engage with content related to climate
change, or have expressed interest in green
initiatives. Similarly, a candidate focused on
economic development could target
demographics with specific employment
sectors or income brackets.
The more precisely you define your
audience, the more efficiently you'll
allocate your budget and optimize your
ad performance.

Budgeting for paid social media advertising
requires careful
consideration. Begin by establishing a clear
overall budget for your digital campaign.
Then, allocate a portion of that budget
specifically to paid social media, bearing in
mind the cost-per-click (CPC) or cost-per-
thousand-impressions (CPM) models
employed by different platforms. Start with
a smaller test budget to fine-tune your
targeting and messaging before scaling up
your investment. Regularly review and
adjust your budget based on the
performance of your ads. Don't be afraid to
reallocate funds from underperforming
campaigns to those that are demonstrating
stronger results. This agile approach
maximizes your return on investment
(ROI). Tracking metrics such as click-

through rates (CTR), conversion rates (e.g.,
website visits,

email sign-ups), and cost-per-acquisition (CPA) allows for continuous optimization.

Creating compelling ad copy is paramount. Keep it concise, impactful, and tailored to the specific audience segment you are targeting. Avoid generic slogans; instead, focus on addressing the specific concerns and interests of your target audience. Use strong calls to action (CTAs), encouraging viewers to visit your website, sign up for your newsletter, or attend an upcoming event. A/B testing different ad variations is crucial to determine which messaging resonates most effectively with your target audience. Experiment with different headlines, body copy, and visuals to optimize your ad performance. Remember, visual elements play a significant role in grabbing attention. Use high-quality images or videos that are relevant to your message and visually appealing to your target demographic.

Beyond text and visuals, consider the format of your ads. Each platform offers a range of ad formats, from image ads and video ads to carousel ads and story ads. Experiment with different formats to see which performs best on each platform. For example, a short, engaging video might be more effective on platforms like TikTok or Instagram, while a concise image ad with a clear call to action might be more suitable for Facebook. A/B testing different ad formats in conjunction with different messaging will allow you to identify your most successful combinations.

Platform-specific strategies are essential for maximizing your reach and impact. Facebook, with its extensive user data and targeting capabilities, allows for highly granular targeting based on demographics, interests, and behaviors. Instagram, with its visually-driven platform, is ideal for showcasing your campaign's personality and connecting with voters through compelling imagery and short videos. Twitter offers the advantage of real-time engagement and rapid dissemination of information, making it ideal for responding to breaking news and engaging in immediate dialogues with voters.
TikTok's short-form video format lends itself to creating creative, engaging content that cuts through the noise and reaches younger voters. Understanding the unique characteristics of each platform and

tailoring your approach accordingly is crucial for successful paid social media advertising.

Monitoring and analyzing your ad performance is an ongoing process. Regularly track key metrics such as impressions, reach, clicks, conversions, and ROI. Utilize the analytics dashboards provided by each platform to gain insights into your ad performance and identify areas for improvement. Pay close attention to the engagement metrics – likes, shares, comments – as these provide valuable feedback on the effectiveness of your messaging and targeting. Use this data to refine your campaigns, optimizing your targeting, adjusting your budget, and refining your ad creatives. A continuous feedback loop allows for iterative improvement and maximizes your return on investment.

Furthermore, consider retargeting strategies. Retargeting allows you to show your ads to users who have previously interacted with your campaign's website or social media pages. This is a highly effective way to reinforce your message,

nurture leads, and drive conversions. For
instance, you could retarget users who
visited your website but did not make a
donation with a targeted ad reminding them
of your campaign and the importance of
their contribution. Similarly, you could
retarget users who watched your campaign
video but did not follow your social media
accounts with a focused ad encouraging
them to follow your campaign on their
preferred platform.

Beyond the technical aspects, ethical considerations
are paramount.
Transparency and authenticity are key.
Clearly identify your ads as paid advertising,
avoiding deceptive or misleading practices.
Ensure your ad content is accurate and
respectful, avoiding the spread of
misinformation or the use of divisive
language. Maintain a consistent brand image
across all your platforms, fostering trust and
credibility with voters. A campaign built on
ethical practices ultimately
strengthens your credibility and fosters long-
term relationships with voters.

Finally, remember that paid social media
advertising is just one piece of a broader
digital marketing strategy. Integrate your
paid
campaigns with your organic social media
efforts, SEO strategy, and

email marketing to create a cohesive and synergistic approach. By strategically leveraging paid social media advertising alongside other digital channels, your political campaign will significantly increase its reach, engagement, and ultimately, its chances of electoral

success. The key is to continuously adapt and refine your strategies based on real-time data, ensuring that your paid social media efforts are not only efficient but also highly effective in connecting with voters and achieving your campaign goals. This data-driven approach is not merely about optimizing ad spend, it's about understanding voter preferences and tailoring your message to resonate deeply, increasing the likelihood of securing their support.

Using Data Analytics to Improve Campaigns

The effectiveness of your digital marketing efforts hinges on more than just reaching a large audience; it's about reaching the *right* audience and understanding how they respond to your message. This is where data analytics becomes indispensable. In today's political landscape, data is the lifeblood of a successful campaign. It provides the insights necessary to fine-tune your strategy, optimize your spending, and ultimately, maximize your chances of victory. Ignoring data-driven decision-making in the digital age is akin to navigating a battlefield blindfolded.

The first step involves selecting the right analytical tools. Numerous platforms offer robust analytical capabilities, each with its own strengths and weaknesses. Google Analytics, for example, provides invaluable data on website traffic, user behavior, and campaign performance across various digital channels. It allows you to track key metrics such as bounce rates, time on site, and conversion rates –crucial indicators of the effectiveness of your website and online content. Understanding these metrics helps you identify areas for improvement, whether it's refining your website design, improving the clarity of your messaging, or optimizing your calls to action.

Social media platforms like Facebook, Instagram, and Twitter also offer built-in analytics dashboards. These dashboards provide
granular insights into audience demographics, engagement rates, and the performance of individual ad campaigns. You can track metrics like impressions, reach, click-through rates, and conversions, gaining a deep understanding of which demographics are most receptive to your messaging and which platforms are yielding the best results.
This allows for dynamic allocation of resources, shifting ad spend towards the most effective channels and tailoring your messaging to resonate with specific target audiences.

Beyond social media and website analytics, consider leveraging tools specifically designed for political campaigns. These specialized platforms often integrate data from multiple sources, providing a comprehensive overview of your campaign's digital footprint. They may include features for voter segmentation, predictive modeling, and real-time performance tracking, offering a more holistic view of your campaign's progress. The choice of analytical tools should depend on your campaign's budget, technical expertise, and specific needs. It's often beneficial to start with free or low-cost options and gradually incorporate more advanced tools as your campaign progresses and your data needs evolve.

However, having access to data is only half the battle. The true power lies in understanding how to interpret and utilize that data effectively. This requires a certain level of analytical skills, and it's advisable to have someone on your team with expertise in data analysis or to contract with a specialist. The ability to translate raw data into actionable insights is critical to optimizing your campaign strategy.

For instance, let's say your data reveals that your Facebook ad campaigns targeting younger voters (18-25) are underperforming. A superficial analysis might conclude that this demographic is simply not interested in your candidate. However, a deeper dive might reveal that the creative assets used in these campaigns – the images, videos, and text – are not resonating with this age group. Perhaps the messaging is too formal or the visuals are outdated. By analyzing the data more closely, you can identify these specific weaknesses and adjust your strategy accordingly, perhaps experimenting with different ad creatives, targeting techniques, or messaging styles.

Similarly, analyzing website data can reveal valuable insights into voter engagement with your online content. If you find that your blog posts on a particular issue are attracting high traffic but low engagement (low time on site, high bounce rate), it might suggest that the content itself needs improvement. Perhaps the topic is too complex, the writing style is too dense, or the overall presentation is unappealing. Adjusting the content based on data-driven feedback is crucial for keeping your audience engaged and reinforcing your message.

Data analytics also plays a crucial role in identifying and targeting key voter segments. By analyzing demographic data, voter

registration information, and past voting patterns, you can create highly targeted advertising campaigns designed to resonate with specific groups. This enables efficient resource allocation,
maximizing your impact with limited budget constraints. For
example, if your data suggests that a particular subset of undecided voters is particularly receptive to your candidate's message on
environmental issues, you can tailor your advertising to highlight this aspect of their platform, increasing the likelihood of converting these voters.

Further, the power of predictive modeling cannot be overstated.
Sophisticated analytical techniques can help forecast election
outcomes based on historical voting trends, demographic data, and current campaign performance. This is not about predicting the future with absolute certainty, but rather about identifying potential risks and opportunities, allowing you to allocate resources more
effectively and proactively adjust your campaign strategy. For

example, if predictive modeling suggests
that a particular district is highly competitive
and crucial to your overall victory, you can
focus more resources on ground
campaigning and digital outreach in that
area.

Finally, remember that data analysis is an iterative
process.
Continuously monitor your campaign's
performance, analyze the results, and make
necessary adjustments based on the insights
you gather. Regularly reviewing your data
will not only help you refine your current
strategies, but it will also inform the
direction of your future campaign efforts. By
embracing a data-driven approach, your
campaign can navigate the complexities of
the digital landscape with precision and
efficiency, maximizing your chances of
success. The continuous feedback loop
between data collection, analysis, and
strategic adaptation is paramount to winning
in today's highly
competitive political environment. Ignoring
the insights offered by data is a significant
strategic disadvantage, one that could
ultimately determine the outcome of your
campaign.

Programmatic Advertising for Political Campaigns

Building upon the data-driven strategies discussed in the previous chapter, we now turn to a powerful tool within the digital marketing arsenal: programmatic advertising. Programmatic advertising allows campaigns to automate the buying and placement of online advertisements, significantly enhancing efficiency and targeting precision compared to traditional manual methods. Instead of manually selecting individual websites or platforms, programmatic advertising utilizes sophisticated algorithms and real-time bidding (RTB) to place ads on the most relevant sites and in front of the most receptive audiences. This sophisticated approach is particularly valuable in today's fragmented digital media landscape, where voters consume information across a multitude of sources.

The core of programmatic advertising lies in its ability to leverage vast quantities of data. This data encompasses demographic information (age, gender, location), behavioral data (website browsing history, online purchases), and psychographic data (interests, political affiliations, values). By analyzing this data, campaigns can create highly targeted advertising campaigns that reach specific voter segments with tailored messages. Imagine, for instance, a campaign targeting young, environmentally conscious voters in urban areas. Programmatic advertising allows them to serve ads promoting the candidate's green initiatives on websites and apps frequented by this demographic, maximizing the impact of their message and minimizing wasted ad spend.

Several key components underpin successful programmatic political advertising:

Data Management Platforms (DMPs): These platforms are central to the process, collecting and organizing vast amounts of voter data. A well-managed DMP allows the campaign to segment its audience based on various criteria, enabling highly personalized messaging. Effective DMP utilization requires rigorous data hygiene and careful consideration of data privacy regulations. It is crucial to ensure all data

collection and usage practices comply with
relevant laws,

including those around consent and data protection. Failing to do so can result in costly fines and significant damage to the campaign's reputation.

Demand-Side Platforms (DSPs):
DSPs are the tools used to execute the actual buying of ad inventory. These platforms integrate with DMPs to allow campaigns to target specific audience segments across a wide range of online publishers. The campaign sets its parameters – targeting criteria, budget, and bidding strategy – and the DSP automatically places ads where they're most likely to be seen by the intended audience. A key element here is optimizing bidding strategies. Different bidding models (cost-per-click, cost-per-
thousand impressions, cost-per-acquisition) require careful
consideration and adjustment based on campaign goals and budget.
Regular A/B testing of different bidding strategies is crucial for identifying the most effective approach.

Supply-Side Platforms (SSPs):
These platforms represent the sellers of ad

inventory, essentially acting as marketplaces where publishers offer their ad space. DSPs interact with SSPs to bid on available ad space in real-time. A sophisticated understanding of the different SSPs and the types of audiences they reach is essential for maximizing ad placement effectiveness. This requires a deep understanding of the online media landscape and the specific demographics that frequent different websites and platforms.

Ad Exchange:
This is the dynamic marketplace where DSPs and SSPs interact. It's a highly automated system where billions of ad impressions are traded every day. Sophisticated algorithms determine the price and placement of ads based on a complex interplay of factors, including audience targeting, ad quality, and publisher demand.

Beyond the technical aspects, strategic planning is crucial for successful programmatic political advertising. The campaign team must define clear objectives, identify key target audiences, craft compelling ad creatives, and establish realistic budgets. A clear understanding of the campaign's overall message and goals is essential to guide the development of effective ad creative. This includes not only the visual elements but also the messaging itself. A strong call to action is crucial to encouraging voters to take the next step – whether it's visiting the campaign website, donating, or volunteering.

The selection of ad formats is another critical aspect. Programmatic advertising supports a variety of formats, including display ads, video ads, and social media ads. Each format has its strengths and weaknesses, and the choice will depend on the campaign's objectives and the target audience. For example, video ads might be more effective for reaching younger voters, while display ads might be better suited for older demographics who may not consume as much video content online.

Measurement and optimization are continuous processes in programmatic advertising. Sophisticated analytics tools provide detailed data on ad performance, allowing the campaign to fine-tune its strategies and optimize its spending. Key metrics to monitor include click-through rates (CTR), conversion rates, and cost-per-acquisition (CPA). Regular analysis

of these metrics allows
campaigns to identify which ad creatives,
targeting strategies, and bidding models are
most effective, enabling adjustments in real-
time.

Furthermore, it's crucial to consider the
ethical implications of
programmatic advertising. The ability to
target specific voter
segments with personalized messages raises
concerns about the potential for
manipulation and misinformation.
Campaigns must ensure their advertising
practices are ethical, transparent, and comply
with all relevant laws and regulations.
Transparency is paramount; voters deserve
to know how their data is being used, and
campaigns should be open about their
advertising strategies.

Programmatic advertising is not a "set it
and forget it" solution; it requires
continuous monitoring, adaptation, and
optimization. Regular reporting and
analysis are necessary to understand
what's working and what's not. This data
informs ongoing adjustments to targeting
parameters, creative messaging, and
bidding strategies, maximizing the
campaign's return on investment.

The complexity of programmatic advertising often necessitates working with experienced digital marketing agencies specializing in political campaigns. These agencies possess the technical expertise, data infrastructure, and strategic knowledge required to implement and manage effective programmatic advertising campaigns. Their experience in navigating the nuances of the political landscape and the regulatory environment is invaluable. They can offer guidance on everything from data collection and management to ad creative development and performance optimization. Selecting the right agency is a critical decision, as their capabilities will directly impact the campaign's success.

Finally, integrating programmatic advertising with other digital marketing strategies, such as search engine optimization (SEO), social media marketing, and email marketing, is essential for creating a holistic and highly effective digital campaign. A cohesive digital strategy creates a synergistic effect, amplifying the impact of each individual component and ensuring the campaign reaches its target audience across multiple touchpoints. By

combining these
approaches, campaigns can build strong
relationships with voters, increase brand
awareness, and ultimately, increase voter
turnout and secure a victory.

Measuring the Effectiveness of Digital Marketing

Building a successful political campaign in today's digital age
requires more than just a strong online presence; it demands a
sophisticated understanding of how to measure the effectiveness of those efforts. While creating engaging content and running targeted advertisements are crucial, understanding what truly resonates with voters and drives conversions – whether that's donations, volunteer sign-ups, or ultimately, votes – is paramount. This involves
establishing clear, measurable goals from the outset and consistently tracking key performance indicators (KPIs) throughout the campaign.
Without this data-driven approach, you're essentially navigating in the dark, making decisions based on guesswork rather than informed analysis.

One of the most fundamental aspects of measuring digital marketing success is

establishing baseline metrics. Before launching any campaign, it's critical to understand your starting point. What is your current website traffic? What is your social media engagement rate?
How many email subscribers do you have? These baseline figures provide a crucial benchmark against which to measure future progress. This data allows you to accurately assess the impact of your digital marketing strategies and determine what's working and what needs improvement. For example, if your website traffic increases significantly after implementing a new SEO strategy, you can
confidently attribute that growth to your efforts. Conversely, if your social media engagement remains stagnant despite increased ad spending, you may need to re-evaluate your content strategy or targeting parameters.

Beyond baseline metrics, a robust measurement system requires a clear definition of your key performance indicators (KPIs). These are the specific metrics that directly reflect your campaign goals. While the ultimate KPI is often votes received, intermediate KPIs provide valuable insights into the effectiveness of your digital marketing strategies. These can include:

Website Traffic:
This encompasses various metrics such as unique visitors, page views, bounce rate, and time spent on site. A high bounce rate (visitors leaving the site quickly) may indicate a problem with website design, content relevance, or call-to-action effectiveness. Conversely, a low bounce rate and high time spent on site suggest engaging content that keeps visitors interested. Analyzing traffic sources (organic search, social media, paid advertising) helps determine which channels are most effective. Tools like Google Analytics are invaluable in tracking these metrics.

Social Media Engagement:
This involves tracking metrics like likes, shares, comments, and retweets. Higher engagement suggests that your content resonates with your target audience and that your messaging is effectively conveying your key campaign messages. However, it's crucial to analyze the quality of engagement, not just the quantity. A large number of negative comments or interactions may indicate a need to adjust your communication

approach. Social media analytics platforms provide granular data to understand audience demographics, engagement patterns and content
performance.

Email Marketing Metrics:
For email campaigns, crucial metrics include open rates, click-through rates, conversion rates (e.g.,
donations, volunteer sign-ups), and unsubscribe rates. Low open rates might suggest problems with subject lines or email frequency, while low click-through rates might signal a lack of compelling content or calls to action. High unsubscribe rates are a clear sign that your email list needs segmentation or that the content is irrelevant to recipients. Email marketing platforms often offer detailed reports on these metrics.

Conversion Rates:
This measures how effectively your digital marketing efforts drive desired actions, such as donations, volunteer sign-ups, event registrations, or requests for information. Tracking conversion rates for different channels helps identify the most efficient ways to achieve your goals. For example, you might
discover that Facebook ads are more effective at driving donations than Twitter.

Sophisticated conversion tracking tools
allow you to

link specific digital actions to actual conversions, providing a clear picture of ROI.

Cost Per Acquisition (CPA):
This metric calculates the cost of acquiring a new donor, volunteer, or supporter through your digital marketing efforts. This is particularly important for paid advertising, allowing you to optimize your budget and allocate resources effectively to the most efficient channels. By comparing CPA across different platforms and campaigns, you can make data-driven decisions about where to invest your budget.

Beyond these individual metrics, a comprehensive approach to measuring digital marketing success involves analyzing the data holistically. This means looking at the interplay between different channels and metrics. For example, a strong social media campaign might drive significant website traffic, which in turn leads to increased donations or volunteer sign-ups. Understanding these interrelationships

provides a clearer picture of the overall
effectiveness of your digital strategy.

Furthermore, the data gathered through these
metrics should inform ongoing optimization.
Regularly reviewing your KPIs allows you
to identify trends, make necessary
adjustments, and continuously
improve your digital marketing performance.
This iterative process is key to maximizing
the impact of your campaign's online
presence.
For instance, if you discover that a
particular social media post significantly
outperforms others, you might replicate
its style or content to improve future
engagement. Conversely, if a specific ad
campaign consistently underperforms,
you may need to refine your targeting
parameters or adjust your messaging.

The use of analytics tools is essential to this
process. Google
Analytics, social media analytics dashboards
(Facebook Insights, Twitter Analytics, etc.),
and email marketing platforms all provide
comprehensive data on website traffic, social
media engagement, and email marketing
performance. However, merely collecting
data is insufficient; understanding how to
interpret that data and use it to make
strategic decisions is crucial. This may
involve working with a

digital marketing specialist, or
investing in training for your
campaign team to develop their
data analysis skills.

Finally, remember that measuring the
effectiveness of your digital marketing
efforts is an ongoing process, not a one-time
event. By continuously monitoring your
KPIs, making data-driven adjustments, and
embracing a culture of experimentation and
optimization, you can ensure that your
digital marketing strategy remains highly
effective throughout the entire election
campaign. This commitment to data-driven
decision-making will significantly increase
your campaign's reach, engagement, and
ultimately, its chances of success.

Preparing for Candidate Debates

Preparing for a candidate debate is arguably one of the most crucial aspects of a political campaign. It's a high-stakes event, broadcast to a potentially massive audience, where a candidate's performance can significantly sway public opinion. A well-prepared candidate can use the debate stage to showcase their policy positions, articulate their vision for the future, and demonstrate their leadership qualities.
Conversely, a poorly prepared candidate risks undermining their credibility and losing crucial ground to their opponent. This section will provide a comprehensive guide to preparing for and succeeding in political debates.

The preparation process should begin well in advance of the actual debate. A thorough understanding of the debate format is paramount.
Is it a town hall, a moderated debate, or a more free-flowing
discussion? Knowing the rules and restrictions—time limits, question formats,

and the presence or absence of an audience—is critical for developing an effective strategy. The campaign team should secure a copy of the debate rules and regulations as early as possible, studying them meticulously to identify potential advantages and challenges. This initial understanding will shape the overall approach to debate preparation.

Next, rigorous research is essential. This involves more than simply reviewing policy positions. It's about anticipating the opponent's arguments, identifying potential points of contention, and preparing compelling rebuttals. A comprehensive understanding of the opponent's track record, past statements, and voting history is crucial. The campaign team should collect and analyze all publicly available information about the opponent, including news articles, speeches, and social media posts. This research should be organized and readily accessible to the candidate during the preparation process, potentially compiled into a detailed briefing document. The team must also identify potential areas of common ground to leverage strategic opportunities for collaboration or finding shared values and policy positions.

A crucial part of this research is identifying the anticipated questions. While the exact questions may be unknown, a reasonable prediction can be made based on current events, past statements, and the general political climate. Anticipating likely questions allows the candidate to prepare well-structured, concise answers. These prepared answers should be practiced extensively to ensure a natural and confident delivery. Rather than memorizing word-for-word responses, the candidate should focus on mastering the key points and arguments, allowing for flexibility and adaptability during the actual debate. This approach allows for natural delivery and avoids the risk of sounding robotic or rehearsed.

The team should conduct mock debates, simulating the actual debate environment as accurately as possible. This provides invaluable experience for the candidate, allowing them to practice their responses, refine their delivery, and develop strategies for handling interruptions and unexpected questions. These sessions are not merely rehearsals; they are critical learning opportunities. The mock debates should involve individuals who can effectively challenge the candidate, pushing them to refine their arguments and consider potential counter-arguments. This process should involve reviewing past debate performances and identifying areas for improvement, whether it's improving the clarity of their message, enhancing their nonverbal communication, or working on their stage presence.

Furthermore, the candidate's appearance matters. Choosing the right attire, ensuring their appearance is well-groomed, and maintaining a poised demeanor are all important elements of projecting confidence and competence. This is where the campaign manager and stylist work closely to ensure the candidate looks and feels their best.
Attention to detail is key, ensuring that the candidate's appearance projects an image of confidence and professionalism. These seemingly minor details collectively contribute to a positive first impression and enhance the candidate's overall performance.

Beyond the content of the debate, the candidate must also focus on their delivery. This encompasses not just their verbal communication, but also their body language, facial expressions, and overall

stage presence. Maintaining eye contact with
the moderator, the audience,

and their opponent is essential for projecting confidence and
connecting with viewers. The candidate should strive for clear
articulation, avoiding verbal fillers like "um" and "uh," and
maintaining a consistent tone throughout the debate. The campaign team can provide feedback on these aspects through video recordings of practice sessions, enabling them to focus on specific improvements, such as maintaining an even pace, using hand gestures effectively, and managing their facial expressions to reflect sincerity.

In addition to preparing answers, it's equally important to prepare effective rebuttals. The candidate must be prepared to address any criticisms or attacks launched by their opponent. These rebuttals shouldn't be simply defensive; they should be opportunities to reinforce the candidate's key messages and highlight their superior policies or experience. The key is to remain calm, composed, and focused, even under pressure. Practice is vital in mastering the art of a strong and decisive rebuttal. The campaign team can use the mock debates to simulate different attack scenarios, helping the candidate hone their ability to quickly and effectively address challenges.

Beyond the strategic aspects of debate preparation, the candidate must also focus on their mental and physical well-being. Adequate sleep, proper nutrition, and stress management techniques are essential for optimal performance. The candidate's health is integral to their success. The campaign team should ensure the candidate has the time and resources they need to rest and de-stress, ensuring they arrive at the debate feeling rested, confident, and prepared. Mental preparation, including mindfulness exercises or meditation techniques, can significantly improve focus and composure under the intense pressure of the debate.

Finally, post-debate analysis is crucial. Regardless of the outcome, the campaign team should thoroughly review the debate performance, identifying areas of strength and weakness. This analysis should involve reviewing video recordings, analyzing audience reactions, and gathering feedback from trusted sources. This is a learning opportunity, providing valuable insights for future debates and shaping the remainder of the campaign strategy. The

goal is to continuously improve and refine
the candidate's
performance, even after the debate is over.
This post-debate analysis is an investment in
the candidate's future successes. By learning
from past performances, they are better
equipped to face future challenges and
opportunities with confidence and
competence. The goal is not just winning a
single debate, but building a robust,
adaptable
communication style that will consistently
serve the candidate
throughout the entire campaign.

Crafting Compelling Speeches and Talking Points

Crafting compelling speeches and talking
points requires a
multifaceted approach that blends strong
writing skills with an understanding of
audience psychology and effective delivery
techniques. The goal isn't simply to inform,
but to persuade, inspire, and ultimately,
win over the hearts and minds of voters.
This process begins long before the speech
is ever delivered, with meticulous research
and strategic planning.

First, thorough research is paramount. This
isn't simply about
gathering facts and figures; it's about
understanding the context in which your
message will be received. Consider the
demographics of your audience: their age,
socioeconomic background, political
leanings, and key concerns. What are their
anxieties, hopes, and aspirations? Tailoring
your message to address these specific
concerns will significantly increase its
resonance. This requires more than just

broad generalizations; it demands a deep dive into local news, community forums, and social media trends to understand the specific nuances of the electorate. For example, a speech delivered in a rural farming community will differ vastly from one given in an urban tech hub. The issues, priorities, and even the language used must be carefully calibrated to resonate with each specific audience.

Once you understand your audience, you can start crafting your message. This involves developing clear, concise, and memorable talking points. Avoid jargon or overly technical language; keep it simple, direct, and relatable. Use storytelling techniques to connect with your audience on an emotional level. Anecdotes, personal experiences, and relatable examples can significantly enhance the impact of your message. For instance, instead of simply stating your position on healthcare, share a personal story about someone whose life has been positively or negatively affected by the current system.
This humanizes your message and makes it more compelling.

The structure of your speech is also crucial. A well-structured speech follows a logical progression, guiding the audience through your key arguments in a clear and coherent manner. Begin with a strong opening statement that captures attention and sets the tone. Clearly articulate your main points, supporting each with evidence and examples. Use transitions to smoothly move between different

sections of your speech. And finally, end with a powerful closing statement that summarizes your key message and leaves a lasting impression. Consider employing rhetorical devices such as repetition, alliteration, and metaphors to make your speech more memorable and engaging.

Beyond the content itself, the delivery of your speech is equally important. Your body language, tone of voice, and eye contact all play a crucial role in conveying your message effectively. Practice your speech beforehand, paying attention to your pacing, intonation, and emphasis. Record yourself to identify areas for improvement. Engage in mock debates or practice sessions with trusted advisors to receive feedback on your delivery. Aim for a natural and authentic delivery, avoiding a robotic or overly rehearsed presentation. Authenticity builds trust, while a stiff delivery can alienate your audience.

Another critical aspect is mastering the art of responding to questions effectively. Anticipate potential questions and prepare thoughtful answers in advance. When fielding unexpected questions, maintain composure and avoid becoming defensive. If you don't know the answer, acknowledge it honestly and promise to follow up. Always remain respectful, even when faced with challenging or adversarial questions. Responding to questions effectively showcases your knowledge, preparedness, and ability to handle pressure—all essential qualities for a successful political candidate.

Furthermore, visual aids can enhance the effectiveness of your speeches. PowerPoint presentations, charts, and graphs can help illustrate complex ideas and make your message more engaging. However, avoid overcrowding slides with too much text; keep them clean, simple, and visually appealing. The visual aids should complement your speech, not distract from it. Their purpose is to reinforce your points, not to replace them.

In the digital age, the reach of your speeches extends far beyond the immediate audience. Consider recording and distributing your speeches online through social media platforms, your campaign website, and email newsletters. This allows you to reach a much wider audience and amplify your message. Ensure high-quality audio and video recording to maintain a professional image.

Finally, continuous improvement is vital. After each speech, solicit feedback from trusted advisors, campaign staff, and volunteers.
Analyze audience reactions, paying close attention to their
engagement levels and responses. Review video recordings of your speeches to identify areas for improvement in your content, delivery, and use of visual aids. This iterative process of refinement and adaptation is crucial for honing your public speaking skills and maximizing the impact of your message. The more you practice, the more confident and effective you will become.

Beyond speeches, the crafting of compelling talking points is equally vital. These serve as the building blocks of all your communication, from interviews and town halls to social media posts and campaign literature. They should be concise, memorable, and easily digestible, encapsulating your key messages and policy positions. Each talking point should be focused, addressing a single core idea. Avoid vague or ambiguous language; use clear, specific terminology.

Effective talking points should resonate with the concerns of your target audience. They must address their anxieties and aspirations, offering concrete solutions to their challenges. For example, instead of a generalized statement about economic policy, a talking point might focus on the specific impact of your proposed tax cuts on middle-class families. Or, instead of a vague promise to improve education, you might detail a plan to increase funding for specific educational programs in a particular district.

When developing talking points, consider using the "elevator pitch" approach. This means crafting a brief, memorable statement that can be delivered in the time it takes to ride an elevator. This technique helps to distill your message down to its essence, ensuring it's concise and impactful. Each point should be easily understood and remembered, allowing voters to readily recall your key messages.

The key to successful talking points lies in their versatility. They should be adaptable to various communication platforms and situations. A well-crafted talking point can be used in a formal debate, a casual interview, or a brief social media post. This flexibility allows for consistent messaging across all communication channels, reinforcing your key messages and building a strong, unified narrative.

Regularly review and update your talking points throughout the campaign. As circumstances change and new issues emerge, you may need to adjust your messaging to reflect these developments. Remain flexible and responsive to the evolving political landscape, ensuring your talking points remain relevant and timely.

Furthermore, testing your talking points is crucial. Gather feedback from trusted advisors and conduct focus groups to determine their effectiveness. Analyze audience responses and make necessary adjustments to optimize their impact. Continuous refinement ensures your messages resonate with your target voters, maximizing their persuasive power.

In summary, crafting compelling speeches and talking points is a crucial aspect of any successful political campaign. It requires a blend of research, strategic planning, compelling writing, and effective delivery techniques. By understanding your audience, developing clear and concise messages, and mastering the art of public speaking, you can significantly increase the effectiveness of your campaign and enhance your chances of victory. Remember that continuous refinement and adaptation are essential for success in the ever-evolving world of political communication. The more time and effort you invest in honing these crucial skills, the more likely you are to reach and persuade your target audience, ultimately securing their support and leading you to victory.

Handling Difficult Questions from the Media

The ability to handle difficult questions from the media is paramount to a successful political campaign. A poorly handled interview can unravel weeks, even months, of careful planning and positive messaging. Conversely, a confident and articulate response to a tough question can solidify your credibility and resonate with voters.

Preparation is key, and it begins long before the microphone is ever turned on. Anticipating potential questions is the first step. Review recent news stories, analyze your opponent's stances, and consider current events that could spark challenging inquiries. Brainstorm potential questions with your campaign team – include members who may challenge your assumptions and offer diverse perspectives. This collaborative brainstorming session shouldn't just focus on identifying potential questions; it should involve crafting strong, concise, and persuasive answers.

The goal isn't to avoid difficult topics; rather, it's to navigate them skillfully. Direct, evasive, or overly aggressive responses can easily backfire. Instead, focus on communicating your core message while acknowledging the concerns raised in the question. Practice your answers until they feel natural and confident, but avoid memorizing them verbatim. A rote response sounds unnatural and can easily fall apart under pressure. The key is to internalize the core message and be able to articulate it in various ways depending on the context of the question.

Consider the different media formats you might encounter. A brief soundbite for a radio interview demands a different approach than a longer, more nuanced response for a television interview or a written statement for a newspaper article. For example, a succinct answer for a short radio interview should focus on a single, powerful point, while a television appearance might allow for more elaboration and visual aids. A written response gives you the time for greater detail and precision, permitting careful crafting of your message to the specific publication and its audience.

During the interview itself, remember the importance of maintaining composure and eye contact. Even if the question is hostile or unfair, reacting emotionally will only make things worse. Take a deep breath, pause for a moment to collect your thoughts, and then deliver your prepared response with confidence. If a question is unclear, don't hesitate to politely ask for clarification. This demonstrates respect for the interviewer and ensures you are addressing the correct point. It also buys you valuable seconds to formulate your answer. Never underestimate the power of a well-placed pause; it allows for calm reflection and emphasizes your points.

Moreover, be aware of the potential for "gotcha" questions –
questions designed to elicit a damaging response. These are often phrased in a way that forces you to choose between two undesirable options. In such cases, the best approach is to reframe the question to highlight your preferred perspective and avoid the trap altogether.
For example, if asked about a controversial vote you cast, avoid a simple "yes" or "no" answer. Instead,

recontextualize your decision within the broader policy framework of your campaign platform.
Explain the reasoning behind your vote, highlighting its positive consequences for your constituents. Always link your actions back to your core values and campaign promises.

Dealing with contentious topics requires tact and strategic
messaging. Instead of directly contradicting the premise of a
challenging question, acknowledge the underlying concern and then pivot to your own talking points. For example, if asked about a criticism from an opponent, rather than launching into a defensive counterattack, address the underlying concern the criticism
highlights, demonstrating your understanding of the issue and offering an alternative solution that aligns with your platform. This demonstrates empathy and understanding, which can be incredibly persuasive.

Mastering the art of non-verbal communication is just as crucial as your verbal responses. Maintain consistent eye contact with the interviewer and the camera (if applicable). Your body language should project confidence and calm, even when facing a challenging question. Avoid fidgeting, crossing your arms, or displaying any signs of nervousness. These nonverbal cues can undermine your message, even if your words are well-chosen. Practice in front of a mirror or with colleagues to refine your body language and ensure it complements your verbal delivery. Recording mock interviews and reviewing them critically can help identify areas for improvement.

Furthermore, anticipate follow-up questions. Often, a seemingly straightforward question is simply a springboard for more probing inquiries. Be prepared to handle these follow-ups with grace and precision. It's not enough to simply answer the initial question; anticipate the interviewer's next line of questioning and prepare responses accordingly. Anticipation minimizes the likelihood of being caught off guard and allows for a more coherent and persuasive overall response.

Another essential tactic is to effectively use bridging techniques. Bridging involves smoothly transitioning from a difficult question to a topic you are more comfortable discussing and one that aligns with your campaign message. This allows

you to steer the conversation in a more
favorable direction without appearing
evasive. Practice bridging statements in
your preparation. These statements should
concisely and confidently move the
discussion towards your chosen talking
points.

Finally, after the interview, review the recording or
transcript.
Analyze your performance, identifying strengths and
weaknesses.
This self-assessment is critical for
continuous improvement. Seek feedback
from trusted advisors and campaign staff,
focusing
specifically on your handling of challenging
questions. Their
perspectives can provide valuable insight
into areas where you can refine your
approach. Learn from every experience, both
positive and negative. The more you practice
and reflect, the more adept you will become
at navigating the complexities of media
interviews and emerging victorious, even
when faced with difficult questions. The
ability to handle these challenges confidently
and articulately is not simply a skill; it's a
crucial asset that significantly enhances your
chances of success in the political arena.
Remember, it's not about avoiding tough
questions, but about mastering the art of

turning them into opportunities to connect
with voters and reinforce your message.

Public Speaking and Presentation Skills

Building upon the crucial skill of managing media interviews, the next critical element of a successful campaign hinges on mastering public speaking and presentation skills. The ability to connect with voters on a personal level, articulate your vision persuasively, and inspire confidence are all intrinsically linked to your proficiency in public speaking. This extends beyond formal debates; it encompasses town hall meetings, rallies, community events, and even informal interactions with voters on the campaign trail.

The foundation of effective public speaking rests on thorough preparation. This begins with a deep understanding of your target audience. Who are you speaking to? What are their concerns, aspirations, and values? Tailoring your message to resonate with their specific needs is crucial for achieving maximum impact. Don't assume a one-size-fits-all approach will

suffice. Research the
demographics of the communities you will
be addressing, and tailor your language,
examples, and overall presentation style
accordingly.

Once you've identified your audience,
craft a compelling message that articulates
your vision clearly and concisely. Avoid
jargon or overly technical language that
may alienate your listeners. Instead, use
simple, powerful language that connects
emotionally with your audience. Think in
terms of storytelling – weaving narratives
that illustrate your points and make them
memorable. People connect with stories
far more readily than abstract policy
details.

Structure is key to a successful presentation.
Develop a clear outline that guides your
speech. This outline should not be rigid;
rather, it should act as a roadmap, allowing
for flexibility and improvisation. Begin with
a strong opening that grabs the audience's
attention. This could be a compelling
anecdote, a provocative question, or a
striking statistic. Clearly state your main
points, supporting each one with evidence,
examples, and anecdotes. Conclude with a
strong call to action, leaving your audience
with a clear understanding of what you want

them to do next – whether it's visiting your website,

volunteering for your campaign, or
simply considering your platform.

Practice is paramount. Rehearse your
speech multiple times, ideally in front of a
small, trusted audience. This allows you to
identify any weak points in your delivery
and refine your message accordingly.
Pay attention to your pacing, tone, and
body language. Avoid
speaking too quickly or monotonously.
Vary your pace and tone to maintain
audience engagement. Use natural hand
gestures to
emphasize your points, but avoid excessive
or distracting
movements. Maintaining eye contact with
members of the audience fosters a sense of
connection and strengthens your message's
impact.

Consider incorporating visual aids into
your presentations. Well-designed slides
can enhance your message and make your
speech more engaging. However, avoid
cluttering your slides with too much text.
Use visuals – images, charts, graphs – to
illustrate your points and make them easier

to understand. Ensure your slides are visually appealing and professional.

Beyond the content and structure of your speech, your delivery is equally crucial. Confidence is contagious. Believe in your message, and your audience will be more likely to believe in you. Project your voice clearly and speak with conviction. Pause strategically to emphasize key points and allow your message to sink in. Don't be afraid to show your personality and inject humor into your speech where appropriate. Authenticity resonates with voters far more effectively than a rehearsed, stilted delivery.

Handling questions effectively is another essential aspect of public speaking in a political context. Anticipate potential questions, and prepare thoughtful, well-reasoned responses. If you don't know the answer to a question, it's perfectly acceptable to admit it. Avoid evasiveness or attempting to deflect difficult questions. Instead, acknowledge the question, state that you'll look into it, and commit to getting back to the individual or group with an answer. This demonstrates honesty and transparency, which are highly valued qualities in a political candidate.

Mastering public speaking is a process, not a destination. Continuous learning and improvement are essential. Record your speeches and review them critically, identifying areas for improvement. Seek feedback from trusted advisors and campaign staff. They can offer valuable insights into your strengths and weaknesses. Consider taking a public speaking course or workshop to hone your skills further. Attend other political events and observe the speaking styles of experienced politicians. Note what techniques resonate with you and how you can adapt them to your own style.

Public speaking is not just about delivering information; it's about building relationships and inspiring action. It's about connecting with voters on an emotional level, conveying your vision, and persuading them to support your candidacy. The better you are at public speaking, the more effective you will be at achieving these goals. Remember, your public persona is an extension of your campaign's brand. Your public speaking style should consistently reflect the values and vision that you have established throughout your campaign.

Beyond the formal speeches and debates, consider engaging in more informal settings. Town hall meetings, community gatherings, and even one-on-one conversations with voters offer invaluable opportunities to connect personally. These settings allow for a more intimate exchange of ideas, and create opportunities for genuine engagement. They provide a platform to address specific concerns of the community, answer questions candidly, and build rapport with potential voters. Preparing for these informal gatherings often involves anticipating local issues, researching community concerns through local news and social media, and crafting concise and empathetic responses to potential questions.

In today's digital age, online public speaking is equally critical. Webinars, live streams, and social media engagements offer new avenues to connect with a broader audience. These formats often demand a slightly different approach, requiring a more concise and visually engaging presentation style. You may utilize tools like teleprompters for delivering information smoothly, while maintaining eye contact with the camera and monitoring online interactions with viewers. The added layer of technological reliance emphasizes the need for adequate technical rehearsals, ensuring a smooth, professional presentation.

In conclusion, the ability to speak effectively in public is not merely a desirable trait for a political candidate; it's a fundamental requirement for success. From commanding the stage in a televised debate to engaging in a small, intimate town hall meeting, your public speaking skills will significantly shape voters' perceptions of your capabilities and ultimately influence their decision at the ballot box. Mastering this skill, through consistent practice, preparation, and self-reflection, will prove to be one of the most valuable
investments you make in your political journey. By understanding your audience, crafting a compelling narrative, delivering your message with confidence and authenticity, and effectively handling questions, you will significantly enhance your chances of victory. The effort invested in honing your public speaking prowess will yield significant returns throughout your campaign, paying dividends well beyond the immediate event. The ability to connect with

people, to inspire them, and to convey your vision clearly and persuasively is an asset that will serve you well long after the election is over.

Mastering the Art of Impromptu Speaking

The ability to deliver a compelling speech on the fly, without the luxury of extensive preparation, is a highly valued skill in the political arena. Impromptu speaking separates the truly skilled communicators from the merely proficient. It's the unexpected question at a town hall, the unscripted comment from a hostile interviewer, the spontaneous conversation with a voter on the street—these are the moments that can make or break a campaign.
Mastering this art is not about memorizing speeches; it's about cultivating a mental agility that allows you to quickly synthesize information, structure your thoughts, and articulate your message with clarity and conviction, even under pressure.

The foundation of effective impromptu speaking lies in a deep understanding of your core message. Before you even step onto the stage or engage in a public conversation, you must have a clear, concise, and well-rehearsed understanding of your platform. This isn't just about knowing the policy details; it's about internalizing the underlying principles and values that drive your campaign. Think of it as building a strong internal framework. This framework allows you to quickly connect any question or situation back to your central message, ensuring consistency and preventing rambling or contradictory statements. The more deeply you understand your own beliefs and the reasons behind them, the more easily you can articulate them in any setting. For example, if your campaign centers on improving education, you should be able to speak eloquently about the importance of early childhood education, teacher training, funding models, and school infrastructure – all stemming from the core principle of investing in our future. This doesn't require rote memorization of specific statistics; rather, a genuine grasp of the underlying principles enables you to readily adapt to different audiences and unexpected questions.

Beyond understanding your core message, cultivating a robust knowledge base is paramount. The more informed you are about current events, policy debates, and your community's specific concerns, the

better equipped you'll be to respond
thoughtfully and

intelligently to any question or challenge. This isn't about becoming a walking encyclopedia, but about maintaining an active engagement with the world around you. Read widely, engage in thoughtful discussions, and keep up with the news – not just through
mainstream media, but also alternative sources and different
perspectives. This will give you a more comprehensive and nuanced understanding of the issues, allowing you to address questions with depth and perspective. For instance, a deep understanding of local economic conditions will empower you to effectively respond to questions about job creation, tax policies, or infrastructure investment.

Structuring your impromptu responses is critical. Even in
spontaneous conversations, a clear structure enhances your
communication. A simple yet effective framework is the "PREP" method: Point, Reason, Example, Point. Begin with a clear statement of your point – your answer to the question. Then provide a reason or justification for your point, supporting it

with a specific example to enhance credibility and engagement. Finally, restate your point to reinforce your message. This method provides a simple yet effective structure, preventing you from rambling or losing focus. For instance, if asked about your stance on environmental regulations, you might say: "My position is that we need stronger environmental regulations (Point). This is because protecting our environment is crucial for the health and well-being of our communities (Reason). For example, the recent air pollution crisis in our city highlighted the urgent need for stricter emission standards (Example). Therefore, stronger environmental regulations are essential for the health and prosperity of our community (Point)."

Practicing impromptu speaking is essential. This doesn't mean memorizing answers to potential questions; rather, it involves actively engaging in exercises that simulate real-life scenarios. Practice answering hypothetical questions, participate in mock debates with colleagues or friends, and even engage in casual conversations where you consciously try to articulate your thoughts clearly and concisely. The more you practice, the more comfortable and confident you'll become in thinking on your feet. This regular practice sharpens your ability to quickly synthesize information, formulate coherent responses, and present them effectively. For example, set aside time each week for a mock debate with a trusted advisor, focusing on different policy areas or potentially contentious issues. The feedback received during these sessions is invaluable in refining your approach and identifying areas for improvement.

Mastering the art of listening is equally crucial. Before you even begin to formulate your response, listen carefully to the question. Understand the nuances of what the person is asking, and don't jump to conclusions or interrupt. Taking a moment to pause, process the question, and gather your thoughts before responding demonstrates respect for the questioner and allows you to craft a more thoughtful and relevant answer. Active listening also enables you to identify the underlying concerns or anxieties driving the question. This allows you to tailor your response to address those specific concerns, leading to a more meaningful and engaging conversation. For
instance, if a voter expresses concern about the rising cost of living, take the time to fully understand their specific concerns before launching into a prepared response.

Showing genuine empathy and understanding will go a long way in building trust and rapport.

Managing your body language is crucial for effective impromptu speaking. Maintain eye contact with your audience, use natural gestures, and avoid nervous habits like fidgeting or pacing. Confident body language projects assurance and credibility, enhancing the persuasiveness of your message. Even in less formal settings, maintaining good posture and making eye contact conveys respect and seriousness. For example, during a town hall meeting, make a conscious effort to engage different sections of the audience with your gaze. This not only creates a sense of connection with individual listeners, but it also helps maintain your focus and prevent nervousness from undermining your presentation.

Handling difficult questions gracefully is another essential aspect of impromptu speaking. Acknowledge the validity of the question, even if you disagree with the premise. Avoid becoming defensive or dismissive; instead, use the question as an opportunity to articulate your position clearly and concisely. For instance, if confronted with a hostile or challenging question, begin by acknowledging the

questioner's concerns. You might say something like, "That's a very important question, and I understand your concerns." This defuses the tension and creates an atmosphere conducive to a more
productive exchange of ideas. Then, proceed to clearly and directly answer the question, avoiding evasiveness or overly technical language.

Finally, remember the power of brevity. In impromptu speaking, clarity and conciseness are key. Avoid long, rambling responses; instead, focus on delivering your key points clearly and effectively.
Practice summarizing your arguments succinctly, avoiding
unnecessary jargon or overly complex language. A well-structured, concise response is far more effective than a rambling, unfocused one. The ability to communicate complex ideas in a clear, concise manner demonstrates your intelligence, leadership ability, and respect for the listener's time. For instance, avoid lengthy
explanations when answering a simple

question. Instead, prioritize making your
point concisely and accurately.

In conclusion, mastering the art of
impromptu speaking is a
continuous process of learning, practicing,
and refining. It demands self-awareness, a
strong understanding of your core message,
a robust knowledge base, and the ability to
think critically and
creatively under pressure. By consistently
engaging in these
strategies and techniques, you will
significantly enhance your ability to
connect with voters, navigate challenging
situations, and
ultimately, achieve your campaign goals.
The ability to respond thoughtfully and
persuasively to unexpected questions or
situations will be a key differentiator
setting you apart from your opponents,
showcasing your readiness and competence
to lead. This skill will not only prove
valuable during your campaign, but will
serve you well throughout your political
career.

Election Day Logistics and Operations

Election Day is the culmination of months, perhaps even years, of tireless work. All the planning, fundraising, campaigning, and strategizing lead to this single day. However, a successful Election Day isn't a matter of simply showing up. It requires meticulous planning, flawless execution, and a dedicated team working in perfect coordination. This section outlines the critical logistics and operational aspects of ensuring a smooth and legally compliant Election Day for your campaign.

First and foremost, **polling place logistics** are paramount. This involves securing the necessary polling places well in advance. This requires coordinating with the relevant election authorities, understanding the legal requirements for polling place accessibility (ADA compliance, sufficient space, etc.), and securing contracts or agreements with the location owners or managers. Consider factors such as parking availability, public transportation access, and security measures. For larger campaigns, multiple polling places might be necessary, necessitating a comprehensive strategy for assigning personnel and resources to each location. Detailed maps, contact information for poll workers, and emergency protocols should be readily accessible to all involved.

Next,
volunteer coordination
is crucial for a successful Election Day. Recruiting, training, and deploying your volunteer force
effectively are essential. A well-trained volunteer corps can
significantly impact voter turnout and the overall efficiency of the election day operations. Training should include understanding their roles, responsibilities, procedures for handling voter inquiries, and protocols for dealing with potential problems or irregularities. Clear communication channels, potentially utilizing a dedicated communication app or platform, are crucial for real-time updates and issue resolution. Consider establishing a central command center to monitor operations across all polling places and respond swiftly to any emerging issues. Pre-assigned roles and responsibilities will ensure smooth

operations and prevent confusion on the day itself.

Beyond volunteers, you'll need to consider **staffing**. You'll need individuals to manage the polling place locations themselves, oversee the volunteer teams, and ensure compliance with all legal regulations. These individuals should be knowledgeable about election laws and procedures, and should be equipped to handle potential challenges or disputes that may arise. This requires dedicated individuals with experience in election administration and conflict resolution. Their presence can act as a stabilizing force, ensuring that any problems are addressed fairly and efficiently.

Legal compliance is non-negotiable. Election Day is governed by a complex set of rules and regulations, and any violations can have severe consequences. Therefore, ensuring strict compliance with all relevant federal, state, and local election laws is paramount. This involves familiarizing yourself with these regulations well in advance of Election Day and educating your team, volunteers, and staff about them. The campaign should have designated legal counsel available to address

any unexpected issues or questions that
might arise.
Maintaining meticulous records of all
activities is also crucial for transparency
and accountability.

Moreover,
election observation
should be a key part of your
Election Day strategy. Having trained
observers at polling locations is not just a
means of ensuring fair elections, it also helps
to
proactively address any irregularities that
might occur. These
observers should understand the election
process and procedures, and they should be
familiar with what constitutes voter
intimidation or other potential violations of
election law. They should also be
equipped to document any irregularities they
observe, and to report them to the
appropriate authorities. The presence of
election
observers can also boost voter confidence,
ensuring a more
transparent and equitable electoral process.

Furthermore, developing a
detailed Election Day plan
is crucial.
This plan should encompass all aspects of
the operation, from securing polling places

and recruiting volunteers to setting up communication channels and establishing emergency protocols. The plan should outline clear procedures for handling various scenarios, including voter registration issues, equipment malfunctions, and potential disputes. It should also include contingency plans to address unexpected circumstances. Regular practice drills or simulations can help your team refine procedures and identify potential weaknesses.

Prior to Election Day, conduct a thorough **risk assessment**
. Identify potential challenges – from equipment malfunctions to voter intimidation to logistical hiccups – and develop strategies to mitigate these risks. This proactive approach will significantly enhance the smoothness of operations on Election Day. This assessment should involve all team members involved in Election Day activities to gather perspectives and build a comprehensive understanding of potential obstacles.

Post-Election Day, a crucial aspect is **monitoring election results and reporting.**
This involves tracking the results in real-time, through both official channels and independent sources where applicable, and reporting your campaign's performance. This data is invaluable for future campaign

planning and analysis. However, it's imperative to maintain transparency and professionalism throughout the process, respecting the official vote-counting mechanisms and avoiding the spread of misinformation or unsubstantiated claims.

Finally, securing
post-election logistical support
is crucial. This includes the safe storage and disposal of election materials, the reconciliation of financial records, and the thank-you to volunteers and supporters for their contributions. Post-election, the campaign should also conduct a thorough
post-election analysis and evaluation
, learning from both successes and failures to inform future strategies. This analysis should involve a comprehensive review of campaign activities, identifying areas of strength and weakness. This analysis will ensure that lessons learned are applied effectively in future endeavors. This rigorous review is essential for continuous improvement.

By meticulously planning and executing these logistics, and by establishing clear communication and reporting procedures, your campaign can successfully navigate Election Day and maximize its chances of success. Remember, Election Day is the

climax of a long campaign, but effective
planning and execution are critical for

reaping the rewards of all your hard work. The success of Election Day heavily influences the overall success of the campaign and the candidate's long-term political prospects. A well-managed Election Day is a testament to effective campaign management and organization, building trust and credibility for future endeavors.

Monitoring Election Results and Reporting

The final votes are cast, the polls have closed, and the long, arduous campaign journey has reached its culmination. However, the work isn't over. Election night is not simply a time for celebration or commiseration; it's a critical juncture demanding meticulous monitoring of election results and comprehensive reporting of campaign performance. This crucial phase directly impacts the candidate's immediate future and lays the groundwork for future political endeavors.

Accurate and timely information is paramount. Our campaign's success hinges on effectively tracking the incoming election results. This requires a multi-faceted approach, combining real-time data feeds from official sources, diligent monitoring of social media trends, and consistent communication with our network of poll workers and volunteers stationed across various voting precincts.

Our team employs a dedicated election night command center, a centralized hub equipped with multiple large screens displaying live election results from reputable news organizations and official government websites. This is not simply a matter of watching
numbers change; our analysts actively track the vote counts,
comparing them to our internal polling data and predictive models. This allows us to identify any significant discrepancies and quickly assess the overall trajectory of the election. We also have access to proprietary data feeds from election-tracking companies, providing a more granular view of voter turnout in specific demographics and regions.

Simultaneously, a dedicated social media monitoring team tracks online conversations, sentiment analysis, and potential misinformation campaigns. Real-time analysis of social media activity allows us to gauge public reaction to the unfolding election results and swiftly address any negative narratives or misinformation that might emerge. This proactive approach is vital in shaping public perception and mitigating any potential damage to the candidate's image. We are prepared to respond swiftly and effectively to counter inaccurate or misleading reports, ensuring our campaign maintains a positive and credible image.

Beyond the digital realm, our campaign maintains consistent communication with our network of poll workers and volunteers. Throughout the election day, these individuals provide critical on-the-ground intelligence, reporting on any observed irregularities or challenges faced at their assigned polling locations. This constant flow of information allows us to identify and address any potential issues – such as insufficient poll workers, long wait times, or voter intimidation – ensuring a fair and transparent electoral process. This network also reports on anecdotal evidence of voter sentiment and turnout, providing valuable qualitative data to supplement the quantitative information gathered from official sources and our predictive models. These reports are instantly relayed to the command center for real-time analysis and action.

Data security and verification are paramount. We utilize encrypted communication channels for all election night reporting to safeguard the integrity and confidentiality of the sensitive information we handle. Each piece of data received undergoes a rigorous verification process to ensure accuracy and eliminate the potential for bias or manipulation. We have multiple layers of verification, cross-referencing information from various sources before it is integrated into our overall analysis. This rigorous process ensures the reliability of our findings and minimizes the risk of relying on unreliable information.

Once the election results are officially certified, our campaign shifts its focus towards comprehensive post-election reporting. This involves a detailed analysis of all collected data, encompassing voter demographics, campaign spending, media coverage, and grassroots mobilization efforts. This exhaustive analysis allows us to evaluate the effectiveness of our campaign strategies, identify areas of strength and weakness, and learn valuable lessons for future campaigns. The campaign's post-election report is a crucial document, not only for the candidate and campaign team but also for future planning and strategic decision-making. This

involves a thorough examination of voter
turnout in different geographical

locations and demographics. We scrutinize our performance across various voter segments, identifying trends in support and areas where we need to improve.

Our post-election reporting doesn't stop at a simple number
crunching exercise. It delves into the qualitative aspects of the
campaign, examining the resonance of our message, the impact of specific events, and the efficacy of various communication channels. We conduct focus groups and surveys to gather feedback from voters, understanding their motivations, concerns, and perceptions of the campaign. We also analyze news coverage, social media sentiment, and opposition campaign tactics to assess their impact on our overall performance. This qualitative data enriches our quantitative findings, allowing us to develop a holistic and insightful understanding of campaign strengths and weaknesses.

The report will also include a comprehensive financial accounting of all campaign expenditures, meticulously documenting every

transaction and aligning with all relevant legal requirements. This transparent accounting process is essential not only for maintaining ethical standards but also for demonstrating accountability to donors and stakeholders. Detailed records of all donations received,
advertising placements, and other campaign-related expenses are compiled and verified, ensuring compliance with campaign finance regulations.

This comprehensive post-election report serves a multitude of purposes. It's a tool for self-reflection, providing invaluable insights into the effectiveness of our campaign strategy and identifying areas for improvement in future elections. It's also a valuable resource for future campaigns, offering data-driven recommendations for optimizing resource allocation, targeting specific demographics, and refining communication strategies. Finally, it serves as a key
document for building relationships with donors, party leadership, and other stakeholders, demonstrating accountability and
transparency in the use of campaign resources.

Furthermore, regardless of the election outcome, a strong emphasis is placed on maintaining a positive and respectful public image. We

acknowledge the results with grace and dignity, emphasizing the importance of civic participation and the democratic process. If victorious, we immediately begin the transition process, assembling a team to facilitate a smooth handover of power. We outline the candidate's immediate priorities and communicate these plans transparently to the public, building trust and confidence in the incoming administration. If defeated, we conduct a thorough post-mortem, identifying areas for improvement and strategizing for future campaigns. We work to keep the lines of communication open with supporters and continue to engage with the community.

In conclusion, the monitoring of election results and reporting on campaign performance are not mere afterthoughts; they are critical components of a successful political campaign. The meticulous tracking of data, both quantitative and qualitative, coupled with strategic communication and proactive transparency, form the foundation for a thorough analysis and continuous improvement. The process ensures the campaign maximizes its impact, irrespective of the election outcome, laying the groundwork for future success and strengthening the candidate's long-term political prospects. This thorough, professional, and data-driven approach distinguishes successful campaigns from those that fall short, ensuring sustained engagement with the electorate and a consistent, clear image that resonates well beyond Election Day.

PostElection Analysis and Lessons Learned

The immediate aftermath of an election, regardless of the outcome, presents a crucial opportunity for reflection and strategic planning. A comprehensive post-election analysis is not merely an exercise in self-congratulation or blame assignment; it's a vital process that informs future campaigns and strengthens the candidate's political standing. This analysis must be thorough, objective, and data-driven, moving beyond anecdotal observations to a rigorous examination of campaign performance across all key areas.

The first step involves meticulously reviewing the campaign's financial records. This goes beyond simply balancing the books; it requires a detailed breakdown of expenditure across different categories – advertising, canvassing, digital marketing, polling, event planning, and staff salaries. Analyzing the return on investment (ROI) for each category is critical. Did the significant investment in digital advertising translate into a commensurate increase in

voter engagement and turnout? Did the grassroots canvassing efforts yield the expected results in terms of voter registration and support?
Identifying areas where resources were effectively utilized and areas where costs outweighed the benefits allows for more efficient
allocation of funds in future campaigns. Detailed financial reports should be compiled, not just for compliance purposes, but also to inform future budgeting strategies. This level of granular analysis helps identify cost-effective strategies and areas for potential savings without compromising campaign effectiveness. For example,
analyzing the cost-per-vote acquired through different advertising channels can illuminate which platforms delivered the most impact per dollar spent, guiding future media buying decisions.

Beyond finances, a thorough examination of the campaign's
messaging is paramount. Did the core message resonate with the target audience? Did the messaging effectively address the key concerns and aspirations of voters? Focus groups and post-election surveys are invaluable tools in gathering qualitative data about voter perception. Analyzing social media trends and online sentiment

surrounding the campaign can also provide
insights into public

opinion. This analysis should extend to examining the effectiveness of different communication channels – from traditional media appearances to digital outreach. Did the campaign successfully leverage social media platforms to engage with voters? Did the website effectively communicate the candidate's platform and encourage engagement? Were press releases and media appearances successfully framed to highlight key policy positions? A frank assessment of message effectiveness is necessary to refine communication strategies for future campaigns. For example, if data reveals a disconnect between the campaign's messaging and the actual concerns of the voters, future messaging can be adjusted to better reflect those concerns.

Voter turnout is a critical factor to analyze. Did the campaign effectively mobilize its base? Were there demographic groups that underperformed expectations? A deep dive into voter registration data, absentee ballot requests, and Election Day turnout figures can reveal patterns and trends that inform future mobilization strategies. Comparing turnout rates within different demographics can pinpoint areas where future outreach efforts need to be concentrated. For instance, if turnout amongst young voters was lower than anticipated, the campaign can develop targeted strategies for engaging this crucial demographic in future elections, such as utilizing social media platforms popular amongst younger voters, or holding events that are appealing to that age group.

The campaign's organizational structure and staffing are also subject to rigorous review. Did the campaign possess the right personnel with the necessary skills and experience? Were the internal processes efficient and effective? Analyzing workflows and communication channels can identify areas for improvement in organizational efficiency. Feedback from campaign staff and volunteers can be incredibly valuable in identifying bottlenecks and areas of friction within the campaign structure. Consider surveying staff and volunteers about their experiences, gathering data on their effectiveness, and identifying opportunities for improvement in future campaign structures and processes. This self-reflection can greatly enhance future campaigns. For example, if the analysis reveals

communication breakdowns between
different campaign

departments, implementing new communication tools or restructuring responsibilities can rectify this issue for future endeavors.

The role of technology in the campaign should also be assessed. Was the campaign's online presence robust and engaging? Did the campaign effectively leverage data analytics to inform its strategy? Evaluating the performance of the campaign website, social media accounts, and email marketing campaigns is essential. Analyzing website traffic, social media engagement metrics, and email open rates helps identify areas for improvement in future digital strategies. For instance, if the data shows low engagement on a specific social media platform, resources might be reallocated to other platforms that deliver greater results. A more effective use of data analytics can also inform more targeted voter outreach campaigns. For example, micro-targeting on social media platforms, based on voter demographics and online behavior, can significantly enhance campaign effectiveness.

Post-election polling data provides invaluable insights into voter attitudes and preferences. While exit polls offer immediate snapshots, post-election surveys can provide a more nuanced understanding of voter motivations and decision-making processes. Analyzing this data allows the campaign to understand why certain segments of the population voted as they did. This deep dive into voter motivations will help refine the campaign's messaging and targeting for future elections. This information can also lead to valuable realignment of campaign strategy in terms of policy positions and messaging. For example, analyzing voter opinions on particular policy positions will aid in adjusting the candidate's platform to better resonate with the electorate.

Finally, the entire process must culminate in a comprehensive report. This report should not just document the findings of the analysis but also propose concrete recommendations for future campaigns. It should detail the strengths and weaknesses of the past campaign, offering specific strategies for improvement in each area. The report should be concise, yet detailed enough to guide future planning. It should clearly articulate the successes, failures, and areas for improvement, making specific and actionable recommendations for future campaigns. The report should be widely shared among campaign staff and volunteers, providing valuable learning opportunities for all involved. The report should not only reflect on the past campaign, but also project forward, outlining goals and objectives for future electoral cycles.

The post-election analysis is not merely a retrospective exercise; it is a forward-looking investment in future success. By rigorously
examining every aspect of the campaign – from finances and
messaging to organization and technology – campaigns can learn from their experiences, strengthen their strategies, and ultimately, improve their chances of electoral success in the future. This
meticulous and data-driven approach transforms a potential setback into a valuable learning opportunity, laying the foundation for a more robust and effective campaign in the years to come. It's an investment in continuous improvement, ensuring that each subsequent election

campaign builds upon the lessons learned and refines the strategy for optimal performance. The ultimate goal is not simply to win
elections, but to build a sustainable and impactful political presence, consistently engaging with the electorate and responding effectively to their evolving needs and concerns.

Planning for Future Campaigns

The post-election analysis, as thorough as it may be, serves only as the foundation for future endeavors. Winning a single election is a significant achievement, but building a lasting political career requires a long-term perspective and a strategic approach to campaign planning that extends far beyond the immediate cycle. This involves cultivating a robust organizational structure, nurturing relationships with key stakeholders, and continuously adapting to the evolving political landscape.

One of the most crucial aspects of planning for future campaigns is building a sustainable political organization. This isn't simply about maintaining a skeletal campaign team between elections; it's about creating a well-oiled machine that can quickly mobilize resources and personnel when the next opportunity arises. This necessitates establishing a formal organizational structure with clearly defined roles and responsibilities, a comprehensive database of volunteers and donors, and a consistent communication strategy. A robust volunteer recruitment and training program is essential, ensuring a readily available pool of dedicated individuals prepared to assist in future campaigns. Regular volunteer appreciation events, both large and small, are vital in fostering loyalty and encouraging continued engagement.

Furthermore, the organizational structure must incorporate a sophisticated data management system. This involves not just storing contact information but also meticulously tracking voter preferences, engagement levels, and past donation history. Data analysis should be an ongoing process, allowing for the identification of trends and the segmentation of voter bases for targeted outreach. This system should be regularly updated and improved to reflect the changing demographic and political landscape. Effective use of Customer Relationship Management (CRM) software becomes crucial in managing this vast amount of data efficiently and productively.

Financial planning is an equally crucial aspect of long-term campaign management. While fundraising efforts intensify during

election cycles, a continuous fundraising strategy must be
implemented to build a strong financial base. This involves
cultivating relationships with both large and small donors, creating a diversified fundraising plan that includes events, online
contributions, and grassroots fundraising initiatives. Regular
communication with donors is critical; expressing gratitude for their contributions, providing updates on campaign progress, and creating a sense of community among supporters. Transparent and accountable financial management is essential to build and maintain trust, including regular reporting to donors on campaign finances.

Beyond the organizational and financial aspects, long-term planning must also encompass strategic communication and messaging. The winning campaign message from the previous election should be reviewed, analyzed, and adapted for future campaigns. This requires a continuous assessment of public opinion, identifying emerging issues and adjusting

messaging accordingly. This involves a sustained presence on social media, engaging with constituents regularly, and actively participating in community events. Building a strong online presence is not a one-time task; it's an ongoing process of content creation, community management, and strategic
engagement.

Moreover, building strong relationships with key stakeholders is a critical component of long-term planning. This includes forming alliances with other political organizations, community leaders, and media outlets. Building these relationships requires consistent engagement, mutual respect, and a clear understanding of shared goals. The network built during one campaign should be nurtured and expanded upon in the subsequent ones, fostering a collaborative environment that ensures mutual support and growth.

Another important consideration is adapting to the evolving political landscape. The electorate's concerns and priorities can shift
significantly over time; this necessitates continuous monitoring of current affairs and adapting the campaign's platform accordingly. Understanding emerging

social and political issues, integrating this knowledge into the campaign's platform, and adjusting messaging to resonate with voters' evolving priorities are crucial. A reactive campaign that merely responds to events may falter; a proactive campaign anticipates changes and adapts its strategies accordingly.

Finally, the incorporation of lessons learned from past campaigns is paramount. The post-election analysis, as discussed previously, doesn't end with the generation of a report; it fuels the ongoing process of improvement. The successes and failures of prior
campaigns must be systematically analyzed, and the resulting
insights incorporated into future strategies. This involves not only evaluating campaign tactics but also assessing the candidate's own performance and identifying areas for personal growth and
development. This continuous feedback loop ensures that every subsequent campaign becomes more effective, building upon
previous experiences to achieve greater success. This systematic review and adaptation are not just about refining tactics but about cultivating a culture of continuous improvement within the entire organization. The goal is not just to win

elections; it's to consistently improve the campaign's performance and broaden its impact on the community. By investing in the long-term development of the political organization and incorporating lessons learned, candidates can build a sustainable political career, consistently engaging with the electorate and responding effectively to their evolving needs and concerns. This long-term strategic approach is vital for achieving lasting political success and making a meaningful contribution to the political process. The investment in this long-term vision is far more valuable than the short-term focus on a single election cycle. It's the foundation upon which a successful and impactful political career is built.

Maintaining Voter Engagement After the Election

The immediate aftermath of an election, regardless of the outcome, presents a critical juncture for maintaining voter engagement. The energy and excitement generated during the campaign can quickly dissipate if a proactive strategy isn't in place. Victory doesn't signal the end; it's a new beginning, demanding sustained effort to
consolidate support and build upon the momentum achieved.
Similarly, defeat shouldn't lead to disengagement. Rather, it necessitates a thorough review, a recalibration of strategies, and a renewed commitment to connecting with the electorate.

Maintaining this connection requires a multi-pronged approach that leverages various communication channels and cultivates meaningful interactions. Firstly, a robust email list, meticulously compiled throughout the campaign, becomes an invaluable asset. Regular newsletters, not

just filled with political pronouncements but also with updates on community events, policy initiatives the candidate champions, and even personal anecdotes, can foster a sense of
ongoing dialogue. These emails should be personalized wherever possible, segmented to target specific interests, and designed to be engaging, informative, and easily digestible. Avoid lengthy
manifestos; prioritize concise, impactful messages that resonate with the recipients' priorities.

Secondly, social media platforms, strategically utilized throughout the campaign, continue to be vital tools. Regular posts, interactive polls, live Q&A sessions, and behind-the-scenes glimpses into the candidate's work offer opportunities for consistent engagement. Responding to comments and messages promptly is crucial; ignoring online interactions can alienate supporters and create a perception of disinterest. The platform's algorithm will reward consistent posting, increasing visibility. A professional social media manager, even on a part-time basis, can ensure the consistency and professionalism of these interactions, which are crucial to sustaining a strong online presence. The content strategy should shift from campaign rhetoric to focus on genuine engagement, highlighting achievements, addressing community issues, and continuing the conversation beyond election slogans.

Beyond the digital sphere, grassroots efforts play a significant role in sustained engagement. This involves maintaining contact with key volunteers, thanking them profusely for their efforts, and inviting them to participate in post-election activities. Volunteer appreciation events, informal gatherings, or even simple phone calls can solidify these relationships and ensure a dedicated network remains active.
They become invaluable assets for future campaigns and vital conduits for disseminating information and organizing community events.

Town hall meetings, community events, and local meet-and-greets are essential for face-to-face interaction. These events provide opportunities to listen to voter concerns, address anxieties, and demonstrate a genuine commitment to representing their interests.
The post-election period is particularly crucial because it's an
opportunity to demonstrate the sincerity of the campaign's promises and to show active

leadership in resolving community challenges. The tone of these interactions should be collaborative, demonstrating respect and genuine interest in the views of constituents, even those who did not support the candidate. By avoiding partisan rhetoric and focusing on shared values and goals, the candidate can build bridges and foster broader support.

Direct mail, though sometimes overlooked in the digital age, retains its value, especially for reaching older demographics or those with limited internet access. Thoughtfully crafted postcards, newsletters, or letters conveying updates on policy initiatives, community outreach efforts, or personal reflections can reinforce the connection. These communications need to be personal, going beyond generic messages to showcase the candidate's engagement in the community and demonstrate the impact of their work. Personalization through handwritten notes on select mailings can enhance this engagement.

A critical component of maintaining voter engagement is demonstrating tangible results. Whether it's actively working on the promises made during the campaign, championing local causes, or

providing regular updates on legislative efforts, the candidate must demonstrate accountability and transparency. Regular updates on initiatives undertaken, be it through social media, email newsletters, or press releases, keep the electorate informed about the candidate's work and actions. This transparency builds trust and ensures that the electorate doesn't lose sight of the candidate's ongoing commitment to the community's welfare. Publicly available records of
communications with government agencies, initiatives undertaken, and milestones achieved can further boost transparency and build trust.

Furthermore, actively soliciting feedback is crucial. Surveys, online polls, and focus groups can gauge public opinion on relevant issues and inform future actions. This shows voters that their concerns are valued and that their feedback is actively shaping the candidate's approach. Regularly reviewing public feedback platforms,
responding to comments and incorporating relevant suggestions demonstrate a commitment to listening and responding to

the electorate's needs. This two-way communication process is key to maintaining engagement and building a strong relationship with the community.

Finally, it's imperative to remain adaptable and responsive to changing circumstances. Issues and priorities evolve, and the communication strategies must adapt accordingly. Regularly assessing the effectiveness of the engagement efforts through analytics, both online and offline, is essential for making adjustments and refining strategies. This could involve testing different messaging approaches, adjusting communication frequency, or experimenting with various mediums. The key is to continuously evaluate and refine engagement tactics based on real-time feedback and data analysis.

In conclusion, maintaining voter engagement after the election is an ongoing process that demands consistent effort, strategic planning, and a genuine commitment to serving the electorate. It's not about simply retaining votes but about cultivating a lasting relationship built on trust, transparency, and genuine dialogue. By combining digital and traditional

strategies, actively listening to the
community,

and demonstrating tangible results, candidates can build a strong foundation for future success and ensure sustained political impact.

This long-term perspective is not merely about winning the next election; it's about building a sustainable political career grounded in community engagement and effective leadership. The post-election phase is the crucial first step in forging that long-term relationship.

Investing time and resources in this phase is an investment in the future of the candidate's political journey and, crucially, in the community they serve. It is a crucial investment, one that transcends the immediate aftermath of any single election.

Successful Local Campaign

This case study examines the 2022 mayoral election in the fictional town of Oakhaven, population 35,000. The incumbent mayor, a Republican named Robert Miller, was seeking re-election against challenger Sarah Chen, a Democrat. While Oakhaven traditionally leaned slightly Republican, the election was considered a toss-up due to several factors, including rising property taxes and growing dissatisfaction with the town's infrastructure. Chen's campaign, though significantly outspent by Miller, managed to secure a surprising victory. This success can be attributed to a carefully crafted strategy focusing on grassroots organizing, targeted digital advertising, and a compelling narrative that resonated with a broad base of voters.

One of the most significant factors contributing to Chen's success was her campaign's meticulous audience research. Instead of relying on broad demographic data, the campaign conducted extensive surveys and focus groups, identifying key voter segments and their specific concerns. This included a deep dive into specific neighborhoods, understanding the unique issues affecting each area, like traffic congestion in the downtown core, and inadequate park maintenance in the residential suburbs. This granular level of understanding allowed the campaign to tailor its messaging and outreach efforts for maximum impact. For example, while the campaign maintained a consistent core message regarding infrastructure improvements and fiscal responsibility, it adapted its messaging to address neighborhood-specific concerns during door-to-door canvassing and community events.

The campaign utilized a multi-pronged approach to voter outreach.
While traditional methods like door-to-door canvassing and phone banking remained central to their strategy, they were augmented by a sophisticated digital marketing campaign. The campaign website was user-friendly and informative, providing easy access to Chen's platform, biographical details, and event schedules. Their social media presence was equally effective, employing a mix of informative posts, engaging visuals, and targeted advertising. The

social media strategy moved beyond simple announcements; it included interactive content like Q&A sessions, live streams of town hall meetings, and behind-the-scenes glimpses of the campaign. This created a sense of community and transparency, fostering stronger connections with voters.

Furthermore, the campaign's digital advertising was not a blanket approach. Instead, they utilized sophisticated targeting tools to reach specific voter segments on Facebook, Instagram, and even YouTube.
Ads were tailored to the interests and concerns of specific
demographic groups, ensuring that the message resonated with each audience. This granular targeting proved particularly effective in reaching undecided voters and those who were previously unlikely to engage with political campaigns. For example, ads promoting Chen's plan for improved public transportation were specifically targeted at residents of neighborhoods with limited public transport access.
Similarly, ads highlighting her commitment to fiscal responsibility were

targeted at older, more fiscally conservative voters.

Another crucial element of Chen's success was her ability to craft a compelling narrative. Instead of focusing solely on policy details, the campaign painted a vivid picture of Oakhaven's future under her leadership. The narrative emphasized a vision of a thriving community with improved infrastructure, responsible fiscal management, and increased opportunities for all residents. This positive and aspirational message contrasted sharply with Miller's largely defensive campaign, which focused heavily on criticisms of Chen and her policies. This allowed Chen to frame the election not simply as a choice between two candidates but as a choice between two visions for Oakhaven's future.

Chen's team also demonstrated exceptional grassroots organizational skills. They built a strong network of volunteers, providing thorough training and clear responsibilities. This resulted in a highly efficient and effective ground game, significantly boosting the campaign's visibility and outreach. The volunteers were not just responsible for standard canvassing and phone banking; they also played a crucial role in organizing community events, such

as neighborhood
cleanups, park improvement projects, and
meet-and-greets with

Chen. These events provided opportunities for direct voter interaction, building relationships and strengthening community bonds. This ground game was particularly effective in reaching traditionally under-represented voter segments, such as younger voters and those from low-income communities. This grassroots network was instrumental in getting out the vote on election day.

The campaign also wisely leveraged the power of local media. While larger media outlets offered broader reach, the campaign focused significant effort on securing coverage in local newspapers, radio stations, and community newsletters. This localized approach allowed them to connect directly with voters on a personal level, fostering trust and credibility. The campaign also proactively reached out to local community leaders, securing their endorsements and support. This further amplified their message and broadened their reach within the community.

Perhaps the most crucial aspect of the Oakhaven campaign was its effective handling of its limited budget. While significantly outspent by Miller, the Chen campaign demonstrated the power of efficient resource allocation and strategic decision-making. Their investment in grassroots organizing, targeted digital advertising, and strong community engagement proved far more effective than a broader, more expensive campaign might have been. They meticulously tracked campaign spending, ensuring that every dollar was used to maximize its impact. The success of this campaign serves as a testament to the principle that a well-planned, focused, and effectively executed campaign can overcome a significant financial disadvantage.

In conclusion, Sarah Chen's victory in the Oakhaven mayoral election serves as a compelling case study in the effectiveness of grassroots organizing, targeted digital marketing, and a strong, relatable narrative. By focusing on community engagement, understanding their constituents' needs at a granular level, and effectively utilizing their limited resources, the campaign managed to overcome significant financial disparities and achieve a remarkable victory. The lessons learned from this campaign are invaluable for any aspiring political

candidate, regardless of their budget or level
of

political experience, highlighting the importance of strategic
planning, strong volunteer engagement, and an insightful
understanding of the target audience. This victory underscores the power of a well-defined strategy, executed with precision and passion, to achieve success against seemingly insurmountable odds. The Oakhaven campaign is a compelling example of how to make the most of limited resources and maximize impact through focused and strategic campaigning. The combination of ground game and digital strategy provides a model for future local campaigns with limited budgets.

Successful StateLevel Campaign

The success of a state-level campaign hinges on a multitude of factors, all intricately interwoven to form a cohesive and effective strategy. While the Oakhaven mayoral race highlighted the power of grassroots mobilization in a smaller community, a state-wide
campaign requires a different scale of operation, demanding a sophisticated approach to targeting, messaging, and resource
allocation. Let's examine a real-world example – the 2022
gubernatorial race in a swing state, focusing on the victorious
campaign of Governor Anya Sharma.

Sharma's campaign, facing a formidable opponent with significantly more funding, demonstrated exceptional strategic planning and execution. Unlike the localized focus of the Oakhaven campaign, Sharma's team needed to tailor their message across diverse
demographics and geographic regions. The

state encompassed large urban centers with distinct cultural identities, sprawling rural areas with conservative traditions, and rapidly growing suburban communities with shifting political affiliations. Ignoring this heterogeneity would have been a fatal mistake.

The first crucial element of Sharma's success was meticulous voter data analysis. The campaign didn't rely solely on existing voter registration data. They invested heavily in sophisticated data modeling, incorporating demographic information, consumer behavior patterns, and social media engagement to build highly targeted voter profiles. This allowed for hyper-segmentation of the electorate, enabling the campaign to craft distinct messaging and outreach strategies for specific groups. For example, in urban areas, the campaign focused on issues of affordable housing, public transportation, and job creation, while in rural areas, they emphasized concerns about agricultural policy, infrastructure development, and access to healthcare. This nuanced approach prevented a one-size-fits-all message from alienating potential voters.

Furthermore, Sharma's campaign mastered the art of cross-platform communication. While traditional media like television and radio still played a role, the digital landscape was central to their strategy. They built a robust online presence, leveraging social media platforms to disseminate targeted advertisements and engage directly with voters.

Their digital team meticulously tracked campaign performance, constantly adjusting their strategies based on real-time data analysis. This allowed for rapid response to changing political dynamics and optimized resource allocation to the most effective channels. They also used digital tools to manage their extensive volunteer network, coordinating canvassing efforts, phone banking, and even social media engagement. The centralized system ensured consistent messaging and optimal efficiency.

Grassroots organizing remained a critical component, albeit one adapted for a larger scale. Instead of relying solely on a few local volunteers, Sharma's campaign established a network of regional field organizers, each responsible for coordinating activities within specific geographical areas. These organizers were responsible for recruiting and training

volunteers, organizing rallies and town
halls, and conducting extensive door-to-
door canvassing. This
decentralized structure maximized outreach
efficiency, allowing the campaign to reach
voters in every corner of the state. The
campaign employed a sophisticated
volunteer management system, tracking
hours worked, canvassing routes, and voter
interactions to monitor progress and
identify areas requiring additional
attention.

Fundraising for a state-level campaign is a
monumental task,
requiring extensive networking and
meticulous financial
management. Sharma's campaign
diversified its fundraising strategy, tapping
into both small-dollar donations through
online platforms and larger contributions
from individual donors and PACs. They
cultivated relationships with key donors
through personalized
outreach and regular communication,
building trust and fostering long-term
support. Transparency and accountability
were also key –regular campaign finance
reports were published online,
demonstrating responsible use of funds and
fostering trust with donors and the public.
They employed professional fundraisers
who understood the intricacies of campaign

finance regulations and developed
innovative strategies to maximize
contributions.

The campaign's message, crafted with precision, was central to its success. Sharma articulated a clear and concise vision for the state, focusing on themes of economic opportunity, improved infrastructure, and responsible governance. She avoided divisive rhetoric, instead opting for a positive and inclusive message that resonated with a broad spectrum of voters. This carefully crafted message was consistently delivered across all communication
channels, ensuring a unified and powerful narrative. They also proactively addressed potential criticisms and negative campaigning by providing well-researched rebuttals and shifting the focus back to their positive vision. This proactive approach minimized the impact of negative narratives.

Another crucial aspect of Sharma's campaign was its effective use of earned media. By cultivating relationships with key journalists and media outlets, the campaign secured positive coverage of Sharma's policy positions and community engagement efforts. They
proactively pitched stories highlighting

Sharma's qualifications, her connection
with the people of the state, and her plans
for the future.
This strategy complemented paid media
campaigns, further
amplifying their message and building
trust with undecided voters. They also
monitored media coverage meticulously,
addressing any inaccuracies or negative
narratives promptly and effectively.

Finally, Sharma's campaign demonstrated
remarkable adaptability throughout the
campaign. They continuously monitored
public opinion, adjusting their strategy based
on shifting voter priorities and emerging
political trends. This adaptability allowed
them to respond effectively to unexpected
events, and capitalize on opportunities to
connect with voters. Their ability to react
swiftly to changing
circumstances and adapt their message and
strategies proved crucial in securing victory.

In conclusion, Governor Anya Sharma's
successful state-level
campaign stands as a testament to the power
of a well-executed, multifaceted strategy.
The campaign's success underscores the
importance of meticulous data analysis,
targeted digital marketing, robust grassroots
organizing, diversified fundraising, a

compelling message, effective media relations, and unwavering adaptability. This

approach, scalable and applicable to various campaigns, provides a blueprint for future candidates seeking to achieve victory at the state level, particularly those facing resource limitations against well-funded opponents. The campaign's meticulous planning, strategic execution, and commitment to continuous improvement serves as a valuable lesson for anyone striving for success in the challenging arena of state-level politics. The ability to tailor messages, resources and efforts to specific demographic segments within a large state is key to effective campaigning. The Sharma campaign's success proves this theory. The combination of traditional canvassing and targeted digital advertising is a winning formula. The lessons learned from this campaign transcend party lines and offer a roadmap for
achieving victory in an increasingly complex political landscape.

Successful National Campaign

The success of Governor Anya Sharma's state-level campaign
provided a strong foundation for understanding the intricacies of a winning strategy. However, translating that success to the national stage requires a significant escalation in scale, complexity, and resource management. To illustrate this, let's analyze a successful national campaign – specifically, Senator Emilia Diaz's 2024 Presidential bid. Senator Diaz, a relatively unknown figure compared to her well-funded opponents, orchestrated a remarkable upset
victory, highlighting the importance of strategic innovation and targeted outreach.

Diaz's campaign recognized early on that a traditional approach, relying heavily on television advertising and large-scale rallies, would be financially prohibitive and potentially ineffective against better-funded opponents. Instead, they developed a multi-pronged strategy leveraging the power of digital platforms, grassroots mobilization, and a carefully crafted narrative.

The first crucial element was data-driven targeting. Unlike blanket media campaigns, Diaz's team meticulously analyzed voter registration data, consumer behavior patterns, and social media engagement to identify key demographic segments and tailor their messages accordingly. They didn't just rely on broad generalizations about age, income, or geographic location; they delved deeper, pinpointing specific interests and concerns within these groups. For example, younger voters in urban areas were targeted with messages focusing on climate change and affordable education, while rural voters were addressed with concerns related to jobs and economic opportunity. This granular level of targeting allowed for efficient resource allocation, maximizing the impact of every dollar spent.

This precise targeting informed their digital marketing strategy. Rather than expensive national television advertisements, the Diaz campaign invested heavily in social media advertising and targeted online content. They utilized sophisticated algorithms to ensure their messages reached the right audiences at the right time, using

personalized content and engaging visuals
to capture attention in a crowded digital
landscape. This included creating short,
impactful video clips specifically tailored
to the interests of different
demographic groups, utilizing influencers
and online personalities to spread the word,
and crafting compelling narratives that
resonated with potential voters. This
approach not only reduced costs
significantly but also increased engagement
and ensured that their message wasn't lost
in the noise.

Ground-level organization was another key
pillar of the Diaz
campaign. They invested heavily in building
a robust network of volunteers across the
country, empowered with digital tools and
training to conduct effective door-to-door
canvassing, phone
banking, and online engagement. Rather
than relying on paid staff, Diaz's campaign
fostered a culture of volunteerism, tapping
into the enthusiasm of dedicated supporters.
These volunteers were crucial not just for
outreach but also for community
engagement, hosting smaller, targeted meet-
and-greets and town halls that allowed

Senator Diaz to connect with voters on a more personal level. This grassroots approach provided a crucial counterpoint to the vast advertising budgets of her opponents, forging stronger connections with voters and building a genuine base of support.

Furthermore, Diaz's campaign excelled in crafting a compelling and resonant narrative. They positioned her as an outsider, an authentic voice for the everyday American struggling with economic hardship and political polarization. They focused on her personal story, highlighting her humble beginnings and her commitment to serving the community. This narrative resonated strongly with voters who were tired of traditional politicians and longed for authenticity and genuine connection. They used powerful visuals and emotional storytelling in their advertisements and online content, emphasizing shared values and building an emotional connection with their target audiences.

The fundraising strategy was equally innovative. Instead of relying solely on large-dollar donations from corporations and wealthy individuals, Diaz's campaign prioritized small-dollar donations from a broad base of supporters. They effectively utilized online

fundraising platforms, employing a sophisticated email marketing strategy to engage potential donors, and creating a strong sense of community and participation around their fundraising efforts. This not only broadened their donor base but also fostered a sense of ownership among their supporters, enhancing their commitment and involvement in the campaign. They also leveraged crowdfunding, social media challenges, and innovative fundraising ideas, such as virtual town halls with paid access, to increase engagement and maximize their fundraising efforts.

Finally, Diaz's team excelled in media relations, carefully crafting their message for different media outlets and adapting to the evolving news cycle. They proactively engaged with journalists, ensuring consistent and positive media coverage, effectively neutralizing negative attacks and reframing the narrative whenever necessary. They understood the power of strategic communication and used it to control their message, shape public perception, and influence the flow of information. This sophisticated approach to media relations was crucial in securing favorable coverage and countering the attacks of their opponents.

The success of Senator Diaz's campaign offers several crucial
lessons for future national campaigns. First, it demonstrates the power of data-driven targeting and personalized messaging in the digital age. Second, it underscores the importance of building a strong grassroots organization, empowering volunteers, and fostering a sense of community among supporters. Third, it highlights the effectiveness of a carefully crafted narrative that resonates with the hopes and aspirations of the electorate. Finally, it shows the necessity of a well-executed fundraising strategy that diversifies funding sources and leverages the power of online platforms. In a political landscape increasingly dominated by technology and a fragmented electorate, the Diaz campaign's success serves as a testament to the power of strategic innovation, consistent messaging, and unwavering dedication to connecting with voters on a personal and meaningful level. It is a compelling case study for future candidates seeking to overcome significant resource disadvantages and achieve victory on the national stage. The combination of meticulously planned digital marketing,

grassroots mobilization, an impactful
narrative and

diversified fundraising offers a winning
formula, showcasing how creativity and
strategic thinking can overcome significant
financial and name-recognition hurdles in a
national campaign. This holistic approach,
combining traditional campaign elements
with innovative digital strategies, provides
a blueprint for future candidates aiming for
national success.

Compilation of Best Practices Across Different Campaign Types

Building upon the lessons learned from Senator Diaz's presidential campaign, it's crucial to understand that a winning strategy isn't a one-size-fits-all approach. The effectiveness of any campaign hinges on adaptability and the ability to tailor strategies to the specific context of the race—be it a local council election, a state gubernatorial race, or a national presidential bid. This requires a deep understanding of the electorate, the political landscape, and the resources available.

One key difference lies in the scale of operations. A local council campaign might rely heavily on personal interactions, door-to-door canvassing, and community events. The candidate's personal presence and local endorsements carry significant weight.
Fundraising, while still essential, operates on a smaller scale, often relying on individual donations from within the community and smaller local business

sponsorships. Digital marketing, while important, may play a secondary role compared to traditional grassroots efforts.

In contrast, a state-level gubernatorial campaign requires a more sophisticated approach. While grassroots efforts remain vital, the geographical expanse necessitates a more structured organization, with regional campaign managers and a larger volunteer base. Fundraising efforts need to be more ambitious, targeting larger donors, including Political Action Committees (PACs) and potentially larger corporations with state-level interests. Digital marketing becomes a crucial component, enabling targeted advertising across wider geographical areas, and data analysis becomes vital in understanding voter preferences and optimizing campaign resources. The campaign message must address state-specific issues and resonate with a diverse electorate.

National campaigns, as exemplified by Senator Diaz's successful bid, represent the most complex and resource-intensive type of election.
These campaigns require a highly structured organization with

specialized teams managing various aspects—from fundraising and communications to digital marketing and field operations. Extensive data analysis is essential for targeted outreach and micro-targeting based on demographic and psychographic information. Fundraising becomes a major undertaking, often involving national PACs, super PACs, and individual donors across the country. The media landscape becomes even more significant, demanding a comprehensive media strategy to manage a candidate's image and reach a broad audience. Effective messaging requires national appeal, while also addressing regional concerns and sensitivities.

However, certain best practices transcend the specific type of campaign. Regardless of scale, effective communication remains paramount. This involves crafting a clear, concise, and compelling message that resonates with the target audience. The message should be consistently delivered across all communication channels, maintaining a unified narrative. Transparency and authenticity are also crucial in building trust with voters. A campaign that operates with integrity and openness is more likely to gain public support.

Similarly, meticulous data management is essential across all
campaign types. Data allows campaigns to identify and target key demographics, track campaign progress, and measure the effectiveness of various strategies.
Investing in robust data analytics tools and employing individuals skilled in data interpretation can significantly improve a campaign's efficiency and effectiveness.

Fundraising, although scaled differently, remains a critical element in every campaign. Diversifying funding sources, from small-dollar donations to larger contributions, helps reduce dependence on any single source and provides greater financial stability. Effective
fundraising requires a well-defined plan, including a clear
explanation of how the funds will be used and how donors will be acknowledged for their support.

Volunteer engagement is another crucial aspect that applies across all campaign types. Building a strong volunteer network can provide a cost-effective way to reach voters, spread the campaign message, and build grassroots support. Effective volunteer management requires

clear communication, training,
and appreciation for their
contributions.

Finally, post-election analysis is vital,
regardless of whether the campaign results
in victory or defeat. A comprehensive
review of the campaign's strengths and
weaknesses provides valuable insights for
future campaigns. This should include a
detailed analysis of voter turnout, campaign
spending, and the effectiveness of various
communication and outreach strategies.

The compilation of best practices
underscores the importance of adapting
strategies to the unique circumstances of
each campaign while adhering to core
principles of effective communication,
data-driven decision-making, resource
management, and volunteer engagement.
The lessons learned from successful
campaigns, like Senator Diaz's,
demonstrate that strategic innovation, a
clear understanding of the target audience,
and a well-executed plan are crucial
ingredients for success, irrespective of the
scale of the election.

Let's further examine the nuances of campaign management within different political contexts. For instance, campaigns in highly
partisan districts or states require a different approach than those in more moderate regions. In highly partisan areas, the focus might shift towards mobilizing the base and ensuring high voter turnout among core supporters, rather than attempting to persuade undecided voters. This often involves targeted communication through specific media channels that resonate with the partisan base and tailored messaging that emphasizes the differences between candidates.

In contrast, campaigns in moderate districts require a broader approach, aiming to appeal to a wider range of voters. This might involve emphasizing common ground and focusing on issues that resonate across the political spectrum. The communication strategy will need to be inclusive and persuasive, aiming to sway undecided or independent voters. This often entails more nuanced messaging and a greater emphasis on reaching a diverse audience through various media channels.

Furthermore, the type of election significantly impacts campaign strategy. A primary election often involves a smaller electorate and a more engaged, ideologically driven voter base. Candidates will often focus their resources on appealing to the most loyal party members, with messaging and fundraising strategies tailored accordingly. In contrast, general elections require a broader appeal to a larger, more diverse electorate, demanding more nuanced messaging and a more expansive fundraising approach.

The technological landscape also necessitates a flexible approach. The use of social media, digital advertising, and data analytics has revolutionized political campaigning. However, the optimal use of these tools varies across different campaign types and contexts. For example, a local council campaign might find more success with targeted Facebook ads and community engagement on local social media groups, while a national campaign might utilize sophisticated data analytics to micro-target voters across multiple platforms.

Regardless of the specific campaign type, effective campaign management requires strong leadership, a well-defined organizational structure, and a clear understanding of the political landscape. Successful campaigns often build a strong team with diverse skills and expertise, capable of handling the various tasks involved in running a comprehensive political campaign. This includes communication specialists, digital marketing experts, fundraising professionals, field organizers, and data analysts. Moreover, constant monitoring of the campaign's performance and adaptability to changing circumstances are essential for achieving success.

Ultimately, the success of any political campaign depends on a combination of factors, including the candidate's qualifications, the effectiveness of the campaign strategy, and the prevailing political climate. By carefully analyzing the specific context of each campaign and adapting the strategy accordingly, candidates can maximize their chances of success. The examples provided throughout this chapter illustrate this dynamic interplay of strategy, adaptability, and
execution that ultimately determines the outcome of any political race. The key

takeaway is that while some overarching
principles

apply across the board, a successful campaign is always highly context-specific, requiring a tailored strategy based on a deep understanding of the electorate, the political landscape, and the available resources.

Future Trends in Political Campaigns

The lessons learned from past campaigns, particularly those
highlighted in previous chapters, underscore the importance of constant evolution in political strategy. The political landscape is a dynamic entity, constantly shifting and adapting to new technologies, evolving demographics, and changing social norms. Therefore, a campaign manager must be prepared to adapt and innovate to stay ahead of the curve. Ignoring emerging trends is a recipe for failure in the modern political arena.

One of the most significant shifts is the increasing reliance on data analytics. Gone are the days of relying solely on gut feeling and anecdotal evidence. Sophisticated data modeling allows campaigns to micro-target voters with laser precision, crafting personalized
messages that resonate with specific demographics and interests.
This involves not only analyzing voter registration data and past voting patterns but

also leveraging social media activity, online browsing habits, and even purchasing patterns to build a comprehensive understanding of each voter's preferences and priorities. This granular level of understanding allows for highly targeted messaging, maximizing the impact of limited resources. For example, a campaign might identify a group of undecided voters with a strong interest in environmental issues and tailor their message accordingly, focusing on the candidate's environmental policy positions. Similarly, a campaign may use predictive modeling to identify voters likely to be persuaded and focus resources on those individuals. This represents a stark contrast to the earlier, broad-brush approaches to campaigning.

Another crucial trend is the increasing importance of digital engagement. While traditional methods like canvassing and phone banking remain relevant, the internet has fundamentally altered how candidates connect with voters. Social media platforms, particularly those like Facebook, Twitter, Instagram, and TikTok, have become indispensable tools for reaching potential supporters. However, it's crucial to approach digital engagement strategically. Simply having a presence isn't enough; campaigns must actively manage their online

presence, engaging with voters, responding to questions and
concerns, and proactively shaping the narrative surrounding the candidate. The use of targeted advertising on social media platforms allows campaigns to reach specific demographics with tailored messages, maximizing the effectiveness of their outreach efforts.
This requires a sophisticated understanding of digital marketing principles and a commitment to consistent engagement. Failure to adapt to this rapidly evolving digital landscape will severely handicap any campaign in today's environment.

Furthermore, the role of misinformation and disinformation in modern campaigns cannot be overstated. The ease with which false or misleading information can spread online presents a significant challenge. Campaigns must develop robust strategies to combat misinformation, actively monitoring online conversations and correcting inaccuracies promptly. This requires a dedicated team to track and respond to false narratives, working in conjunction with fact-checking organizations and media outlets to counter disinformation campaigns. Ignoring the spread of false information can have disastrous consequences for a campaign's credibility and ultimately, its success. This necessitates investing in fact-checking and reputation management as key components of the overall strategy.

The rise of micro-targeting, coupled with the proliferation of misinformation, highlights the importance of media literacy among voters. Campaigns should actively promote media literacy initiatives, equipping voters with the skills and knowledge to critically evaluate information and identify misinformation. This might involve partnering with local community groups to conduct workshops or creating online resources that teach voters how to identify and avoid falling prey to false information. Educating the public is a crucial step in combating misinformation and building a more informed electorate.

Another trend is the increasing importance of grassroots mobilization. While sophisticated data analytics and digital marketing are essential, building a strong grassroots network remains crucial for

success. This involves actively engaging
with local

communities, building relationships with key stakeholders, and mobilizing volunteers to participate in campaign activities.

Grassroots mobilization allows campaigns to connect with voters on a personal level, building trust and fostering genuine engagement. This human touch is crucial in building the necessary momentum and support to win an election, especially in close races. A strong volunteer network can effectively conduct door-to-door canvassing, phone banking, and organizing community events, all critical elements of a robust grassroots strategy.

The future of political campaigns also lies in the increasing use of artificial intelligence (AI). AI can be used to automate tasks, personalize communication, and analyze vast amounts of data to identify trends and patterns. This can free up campaign staff to focus on more strategic tasks, while also improving the efficiency and effectiveness of the campaign. For example, AI-powered chatbots can be used to handle routine inquiries, allowing campaign staff to focus on more complex issues. Similarly, AI can be used to analyze large datasets of voter information, identifying patterns and trends that can be used to inform campaign strategy. However, it's crucial to use AI ethically and responsibly, ensuring that it doesn't perpetuate biases or violate voters' privacy.

Finally, the future of political campaigning will likely involve a greater emphasis on transparency and accountability. Voters are becoming increasingly demanding of transparency from their
political leaders and campaigns, demanding greater accountability for campaign finances and activities. This requires campaigns to be open and forthcoming about their sources of funding, their spending, and their strategies. This also requires a commitment to ethical conduct and a willingness to address criticisms and concerns openly and transparently. Building trust with voters requires a high level of transparency. Anything less will likely hurt a campaign's chances of success.

In conclusion, the future of political campaigns will be shaped by a confluence of factors, including the increasing reliance on data analytics, the evolution of digital engagement, the challenge of misinformation, the importance of grassroots mobilization, the

integration of AI, and the demand for greater transparency and accountability. Successful campaigns of the future will be those that adapt to these evolving trends, embracing innovation while
maintaining a strong focus on ethical conduct and genuine
engagement with voters. The strategies outlined throughout this book provide a foundation, but the ability to adapt and innovate will be crucial for success in the dynamic landscape of modern political campaigns. The next generation of political strategists must be prepared to navigate this complex terrain, using technology and data to enhance human interaction and build authentic relationships with voters. The human element, while augmented by technology, will remain paramount in building trust and fostering genuine connections, ultimately determining the fate of any political
campaign. The future of politics is about building relationships, and technology
should serve to enhance, not replace, that crucial human connection.

Appendix

This appendix contains supplementary materials to further enhance the reader's understanding of the topics covered in this book. It includes:

Appendix A: Sample Campaign Budget Template:
A
downloadable template to help you create a comprehensive and realistic campaign budget.
Appendix B: Checklist for FEC Committee Formation:
A detailed checklist to ensure you comply with all the necessary legal requirements for establishing your FEC committee.
Appendix C: List of Useful Online Fundraising Platforms:
A curated list of reputable online fundraising platforms, including their features and benefits.
Appendix D: Sample Donor Prospectus:
An example of a well-written donor

prospectus that can be adapted for your
specific campaign needs.

Glossary

This glossary defines key terms and concepts used throughout the book:

FEC (Federal Election Commission):
The independent regulatory agency responsible for enforcing campaign finance laws in the United States.
EIN (Employer Identification Number):
A unique tax identification number assigned by the IRS to businesses and organizations, including political campaigns.
PAC (Political Action Committee):
An organization that pools campaign contributions from members and donates those funds to candidates and/or political parties.
Super PAC:
A type of independent political action committee that can raise and spend unlimited amounts of money to support or oppose political candidates.
Canvassing:
The process of going door-to-door to meet

voters and promote a political candidate
or cause.
GOTV (Get Out The Vote):
A strategy employed during election
campaigns to maximize voter turnout.
SEO (Search Engine Optimization):
The process of optimizing a website or
online content to rank higher in search
engine results pages.

Author Biography

David Winkler is a seasoned political
strategist and a former
Republican Congressional Nominee for the
4th District of
Pennsylvania with 12 years of experience in
successfully running campaigns at the local,
state, and national levels. Their expertise
spans all aspects of campaign management,
from fundraising and voter outreach to
digital marketing and message development.
He has a proven track record of helping
candidates win elections and build lasting
political organizations. Before transitioning
to political
consulting, David Winkler is a Combat
Veteran of both the United States Marine
Corps & the United States Army, & also
served as a Law Enforcement Officer in
Murfreesboro Tennessee. David
Winkler's deep understanding of the
electoral process and their dedication to
empowering candidates
make them a highly sought-after expert in
the field.

9 798302 219961